Opposites

as Equals

Opposites
as Equals

Standard Differences
between Men and Women

— and How to Resolve Them —

ℭ ℑ

Richard Driscoll, Ph.D.
with Nancy Ann Davis, Ph.D.

Published by
Westside Psychology
Knoxville, Tennessee

Westside Psychology is an imprint of Westside Publishing

ISBN: 978-0-9634126-6-9

Library of Congress Control Number: 2008938492

Categories: Self-help, Relationships, Gender Differences, Chivalry,
    Conflict Management, Marriage, Fatherhood, Evolutionary
    Psychology.

Official website: theOppositeSex.info

1st edition Feb. 2009, titled *You Still Don't Understand*
2nd edition Aug. 2009

To:

Our Parents
Who never knew why it was so hard

May you learn to

laugh louder,

cry harder,

love deeper,

and be more reasonable.

The authors hold *both* sexes in the highest regard, see their strengths and weaknesses, their similarities and differences, and earnestly want each of us to make the very best out of our lives and our relationships."

— Steven Svoboda, in *Transitions*

Contents

The Growing Rift

The relationship revolution and the freedom to choose were supposed to improve the lives of women and promote more equitable relationships for all. Instead, we see a generation of families without fathers, fewer lasting marriages, and increasingly bitter and uncivil relations between men and women. A current survey finds that fully a third of women report being highly resentful of men, while a sixth of men are highly resentful of women.[1]

The fabric of the traditional nuclear family is rapidly unraveling. As of 2008, four in ten American children are born to single women.[2] Add unwed mothers together with custodial moms, and we see that over half of our children will be raised by mothers without the biological father in the primary family. So the matriarchal family is now the norm in our confusing times, while the so-called traditional family of a mother and father together with their children is now merely another alternative lifestyle.

Married men and women are found to be ordinarily better off than those who are single, living together, or formerly married. A solid commitment to a marriage partner introduces meaning and purpose amid the confusion and rootlessness of life. Married men grow out of some of their wild and reckless ways, become more responsible, and are healthier, while married women are safer and better off financially.[3]

Mothers and fathers working together offer a clear advantage over single mothers going it alone. Raising children is always a challenge, and two parents should have about twice the resources for the job as one parent alone. Two heads, two hearts, two sets of hands, and the possibility of two pocketbooks provide a real benefit over just one of each. By almost any measure, children tend to do better with fathers and do worse without them.[4] So the prevalence of fatherless families suggests major social problems as the children grow up and step into the future.

Amid our many wondrous technological advances, our lives should be getting better, easier, and more manageable with each passing generation. Yet many of us struggle to make ends meet, and we report less satisfaction with our relationships and fewer close friends. As trite as it sounds, we are overworked and underloved.

So why now, amid our vast material abundance and newfound freedoms, are our most basic relations coming unglued? Something is going terribly wrong, and few of us understand why or what to do about it. A good share of the answer, as we shall see, lies in the typically different natures of men and women.

CR   ⁊0

Part I.
What Do Men and Women Want?

There will always be a battle between the sexes
because men and women want different things.
Men want women and women want men.

—George Burns

If asked about the nature of men and women in Bora Bora, most of
us would be at a loss. We have never been to Bora Bora, never read
anything about the place, and know nothing of its native customs. But
when asked about the nature of men and women in the Western world,
most of us seem just as lost. Why so? We have all grown up with
mothers and fathers, siblings, relatives, and all manner of friends and
acquaintances of either sex. So why do we so misunderstand our
opposites and understand so little about our own gender?

In an age where sex is passé even to teenagers, the nature of men
and women remains as controversial as ever. Current research shows
highly significant differences between the sexes that are not going away,
and many of them are exactly the opposite of what we expect.

Our onboard programming seems to control not only who we are but also how we understand and misunderstand each other. It is the nature of men and women to conceal some of our qualities and exaggerate others, to overlook the obvious in each other and imagine the improbable, and to insist on seeing what suits our own purposes. As men and women we collude to stage an elaborate costume masquerade in which we chat casually or dance closely cheek to cheek but are not at all who we seem to be. Our choreographies are so convincing even to ourselves, that we get taken in by our own performances and see ourselves as who we pretend to be. It is human nature to consider our masquerades right and proper, and to censure those who sneak a look behind them. *Opposites as Equals* takes us behind the myths and masks so we can see ourselves as we are, pretense and all.

We will see why men are more intrigued by casual sex and tend to be sexual opportunists, but try to conceal it, while women are more choosy. We will see why we expect men to compensate women for sexual favors, while it is improper to acknowledge it and most of us would be readily offended by the mere suggestion.

We will see why women are more easily offended and are more insistent in arguments, but insist that it is not so. We will see why men are more highly stressed in angry confrontations and withdraw to avoid unpleasantries, which women interpret as indifference.

We will see why our moral standards tend to support women and hold men accountable, while most of us consider society to be sexist and unfair to women. We will see why men bond more strongly than women and only appear more independent, while women fold relationships almost twice as often as men while appearing to be more emotionally entangled in them.

We will see why women want to converse about a problem, while men want to fix it and be done with it. We will see why men conceal weaknesses and failings, and why women want men to open up and reveal everything.

We will see how fatherhood provided a cornerstone for human civilization, and why it is now unraveling so easily. Primal moral passions which turned men into fathers now mix with our newfound freedoms and act in reverse—supporting women but condemning men and promoting the current surge of fatherless families.

And much, much more. Each misunderstanding is a potential troublemaker, lurking in the shadows, ready to trip us up or send us in the wrong direction down another blind alleyway.

Once we see what we are programmed to overlook, we can look ahead, plan wisely, and promote brighter futures. We will find the answers behind the masquerades, amidst the real men and women we ought to recognize as ourselves.

Our standard social sciences ideology sees men and women as cookie-cutter copies of one another, and attributes any minor differences to anomalies in experience or to social expectations. In the 1990 bestseller *You Just Don't Understand*, Deborah Tannen argues that gender misunderstanding is the result of growing up in all boy or all girl groups and learning to converse in our gender-peculiar ways. She provides vivid illustrations of how men and women talk past one another, using separate dialects—or genderlects, as she calls them.

Yet the tensions between the sexes go far beyond simple miscommunications. Our differences lie not in a few odd social conventions, but in some of our most profound yearnings which bring men and women together or turn us callously against one another. So long as some of our strongest qualities remain unmentioned, as is too often the case, it is a good guess that the vast majority of us do not understand and never will. Meanwhile, relationships continue to unravel, and the rift between men and women continues to widen.

As *Homo sapiens*,[1] which means "wise humans," we face a challenge to wise up and to use some of that higher intelligence we are so proud of to be more forthright about men and women and to chart a more intelligent course.

Any successful resolution should benefit not just one or the other gender but men and women jointly and about equally. So we reveal about as much room for change for each gender, and provide about as many suggestions for each. You are surely welcome to keep score.

We are obligated to warn you that this apparently innocent book you hold in your hands is forbidden contraband, smuggled in past our politically correct censors and at some personal risk to the authors.

Use it carefully!

1.

The Nature of Lust

All the world's a stage,
And all the men and women merely players.
—William Shakespeare, *As You Like It*

A tomcat is willing to leave his cushy home and travel miles, risking his very life for a hot "date." He will persevere through rain, sleet and snow, like the postman; over hill and over dale, like the caissons of old. He is willing to fight his rivals and have his precious hide slashed up, as the swashbuckling adventurer he is, while fair maiden stays close to home, sees who shows up and who wins the fights, and then befriends the victor.

Male dogs come running from hither and yon when a female is in heat, to snarl, bark, lunge, and intimidate each other, jumping fences, digging under, or forcing their ways through, to reach the hottie with the come-hither signals. The female meanwhile watches, waits, and mates with the frontrunner.

While a grown buck is ordinarily cagey and hangs close to the trees for cover, during mating season he ventures out into the open where hunters prey on his temporary lapse in judgment. Wild boars can be vicious, especially to each other. By one estimate, 40% of adult males are killed each rutting season in lethal fights for the females.

The peacock struts a cumbersome array of tail feathers, to impress the hens, and the hens always choose the dandy with the most impressive fan. A resplendent suitor who can produce such a show and still survive amid predators should contribute superior qualities for her brood of chicks.

The male Northern cardinal sports bright red plumage almost as if by choice, to impress the females, while the females are more muted grays or browns with a few highlights. Red is hardly suitable for camouflage. The bright red plumage makes him easy to spot, like the British Redcoat soldiers in the Revolutionary War, whose colorful jackets seemed to advertise, "Easy target, shoot at me! So what? I am courageous, I can handle it!"

Among birds, the males are often more colorful than their female counterparts. The bright feathers are accounted for by an idiot oxymoron, known as the "handicap advantage."[1] The dandy who sports bright plumage is showing that he has the superior qualities to elude predators regardless of his handicap, and the females who choose the colorful daredevil will carry his superior genes into the next generation.

Are we beginning to see a pattern here? Males seem to be more interested in sex, are more sexually aggressive, and are willing to go farther, sacrifice more, fight harder, and risk more to mate than are females. Regardless of where we look, the pattern continues— among those that plod over the land, fly the skies, or swim the oceans. In every niche and in every climate, across the breadth and variety of species that populate the earth, males pursue and females, as Charles Darwin observed, are somewhat "coy." Obviously, not all females are exactly coy. It is common for females to have multiple partners, and many primate females actively solicit for social and material benefits.[2] It is relative to males—who will typically venture into unfamiliar territories, battle rivals, and risk their very lives for sex—that females are clearly more reserved. The observation is solid and has only grown stronger over a century and a half of close scrutiny.

Human parallels

So, what do lustful animals have to do with men and women? We humans are civilized creatures, so our conduct is shaped and trimmed by our cultures. And yet we are animals as well, specifically primate mammals, and we share many of the physiological features of other animals. Is it possible that we might share some of the behavioral features, too?

Well, surely, if only in just the obvious ways. We forage for food when we are hungry, and we struggle to survive, as do all animals; we raise our young, as do mammals and birds; and we congregate together, as do packs of wolves, prides of lions, troops of monkeys, herds of reindeer, pods of whales, mobs of meerkats, flocks of birds, and gaggles of geese.

Sexuality is among the most sensitive and personal aspects of intimate relationships. How much of its charms and hardships do we share with the plainer animals on the planet? Is it possible that we are driven by our biological programming, more than our social pretensions allow us to admit?

Casual Sex and Relationships

Young men, as most of us realize, are notoriously intrigued by casual liaisons, while young women tend to be concerned about relationships. In just the right circumstances, our inclinations take us on almost entirely opposite paths.

University of Hawaii study

In a study at the University of Hawaii, an attractive interviewer of the opposite sex approached young men and women students, conversed briefly, mentioned having seen the student around campus and finding him or her attractive, and then asked the student either for a date or to go back to an apartment and have sex.[3]

Half of the young men who were asked for a date agreed to go out with the interviewer, as did half of the young women. So college men and women are quite similar in their interest in dating.

Yet there the similarity ends. Of those men invited for casual sex, fully 75% agreed and were ready to go. So more men agreed to casual sex than to dating. Specifically, an additional 25% of college men, not interested enough to date, nonetheless agreed to casual sex. Of those women invited for an anonymous tryst, virtually *none* was willing with such a casual acquaintance.

Even knowing as much about males and females as we do, the 75% to 0% contrast is striking. A full generation after the sexual revolution supposedly freed us from our traditional patterns, we see ourselves here as far apart as we have always been. Should we have imagined that access to birth control and our more liberal sexual customs would have closed more of the gap between us?

Of the 25% of men who did not agree, many were apologetic and asked for a rain check, mentioning a prior commitment or even a fiancée who was visiting from out of town. If not for these prior commitments, the number of men accepting the ruse would have been higher. So interest in strictly casual sex for its own sake may produce the 75% separation or possibly more between the young men and women.

The interviewers who approached the students were impostors, of course, masquerading as admirers who simply happened to find that particular student especially attractive. How gullible we can be, especially young men approached by an attractive woman! The lass with the invitation seemed like an angel and far too good to be true— which of course she was.

Note the irony of the experimental method. We can easily underplay our interests or exaggerate them in an interview. So these researchers had to send in an impostor pretending to be the real thing in order to find out what we would truly do with the real thing instead of what we would merely say we would do when pretending to be candid.

Young men want casual sex

Most university students are away from family and on their own, and the University of Hawaii study may be a fair sampling of what bright young adults would do in a moderately liberal society when they figure nobody is watching. Again and again, in a wide range of situations, we see that men are more interested in casual sex with a variety of partners.[4]

Young men report a much stronger preference "to have sex with anyone I choose" and to have sex with no established relationship.[5]

When asked if you would have sex with an anonymous partner, if there were no risks and no chance of forming a relationship, guess what? Men are four times more likely than women to say they certainly would have sex, and women are two and a half times more likely than men to say they certainly would not.[6]

Is it all right for two people to have sex if they really like each other, even if they've known each other only a very short time? In a 1997 survey, 54% of college men, but only 32% of college women, said yes.[7]

Many women enjoy sex within established relationships, and a few women are as addicted to seduction as the typical man. Responses would differ somewhat, of course, in other cultures. Yet the same basic contrast is found across all cultures, observes anthropologist Donald Symons. It appears in illiterate tribes and industrialized nations, in any climate and any geographic region observed, everywhere in the world.[8] Young men are more eager for sex, while women want to be courted and are more selective.

The University of Hawaii study merely mirrors what we already know about our more familiar casual sexual arrangements between complete strangers—the traditional exchange of hot sex for cold hard cash. Where two meet to barter sex for money, it is almost invariably the man who is interested enough to pay for the service while the woman is willing to go for the money but not willing to go anywhere for free.

Contrasts that emerge clearly in these casual situations may diminish or vanish entirely in other situations. The young men who are so eager for casual sex with a young, attractive woman would not summon the same ardor for a plain woman over fifty. And many of the young women who would reject strictly casual sex with a handsome stranger would be more than willing to go out with him, and then consider sex later as the relationship progressed. Women can be as interested in sex as men but are choosier and consider relationship and social consequences more strongly than men.

Best face forward

Amid modern singles, men and women tend to misrepresent their sexual interest in each other, and in opposite directions. A man wants to know that a woman might be sexually interested in him, to make the chase worthwhile, while a woman wants to know that a man is interested in her for more than just sex, to make the chase worthwhile. So a woman who confesses that she really loves sex can easily arouse a fellow, and she interests him in the chase. In contrast, a man who freely reveals that he really loves sex is just another man on the prowl, and we might even wonder if he is a bit creepy.

So women have reason to present themselves as more sensual than they really are, to make themselves more appealing to men, while men present themselves as interested in more than just sex, to make themselves more appealing to women. We put our best faces forward. We do so to fool our opposites, of course, but we can fool ourselves as well. Is it any wonder that men and women can see themselves as more similar than they really are?

Fantasyland

An average young man will undress with almost any willing young woman, abandoning normal judgment and seemingly oblivious to the consequences to himself or to those he loves. Women find such opportunism hard to understand, or consider it not merely immoral but truly irrational as well. Men see it as poor judgment as well, when they watch some other man take foolish risks or when they themselves are far enough away from their own adventures to look back and grimace. We joke about how a man is "thinking with his little brain instead of his big brain." It's a guy thing.

A man is more easily seduced than a woman. The University of Hawaii study suggests that an attractive woman who has her mind set on seduction may need as little as five minutes to talk a young man into it. It is surely fair to say that men use less judgment than women when getting into sexual involvements. Many men use no judgment at all.

How irrational can a typical man be? Switch the gender positions and look at it the other way around. Suppose a man comes on by telling a woman she turns him on and he wants to have sex with her, and she concludes therefore that he must love her. We would figure that she has no judgment and never had, or that she has just lost all common sense and is temporarily insane. At the minimum, she is a menace to herself and needs to be protected. Now switch it back around. When a woman tells a man he turns her on and she wants to sleep with him, he feels extraordinarily flattered. And yes, at least for the moment, he is so full of himself that he is sure she must be wild about him. He is also temporarily insane, of course. It's a guy thing. But the condition is so typical and so familiar that we try to make allowances and work around it.

 Remind yourself that lust is not a good judge of human character.

Why we stray

Our preferences also contribute to why we are unfaithful.[9] Women who have affairs tend to be unhappy in their marriages, and those who are happy with their husbands tend not to have affairs. Women who stray are often looking for the affection and companionship that is missing in their marriages. In contrast, men who have affairs are *not* found to be more unhappy with their marriages than other men. Men who stray often do so for the thrill of the sex and for the pleasure, but mainly because opportunity presents itself—and not because their marriages are empty or sexually unsatisfying.

A man whose wife is not particularly passionate might think she is seeing another man, which is not necessarily so at all. Women have affairs not so much for the sexual excitement as for the warmth that is missing in a marriage. It's a girl thing. A woman who catches her husband in an affair might figure he is dissatisfied with her, which is not necessarily the case either. Men have affairs not so much because something is missing in the marriage, but for the sexual adventure. It's a guy thing.

When you catch your fellow cheating and he uses the old, lame, "It was just the sex" excuse, realize that, sadly, regardless of the rest of the lies, in this one isolated instance he is probably telling you the truth.

A woman who is angry at her husband is more apt to stray, suggesting that infidelities among women may also be an expression of anger and retribution. A man who is angry at his wife is no more inclined to have an affair than one who is not angry. So a woman typically considers her primary relationship, whereas a man should but typically does not. He should, of course. Did we mention that he should?

 If you catch your wife cheating and you conclude that you have a huge problem on your hands, then for whatever it is worth, you are probably right.

Some men are inclined to be cads, others dads. Yet male genes benefit from what Robert Trivers calls a "mixed reproductive strategy," which we might just as well call a "mixed up" reproductive strategy. Men who marry want to stay to raise their children *and* are intrigued by casual trysts with other women.[10] That is, men are inclined to be dads at home, as expected, and cads elsewhere, as opportunity permits.

Female genes benefit from a committed man who will support the woman and her children, but stand to lose in uncompensated trysts. So, a woman usually wants to know whether a man genuinely loves her and is not just playing. The ways in which women seek commitments, and the reasons men commit, are at the heart of intimate relationships.

Nature Plus Nurture

Do some of the contrasts between men and women proceed from a biological imperative, acting fiercely beneath the surface and streamlining itself into our conscious minds?

Origins of sexual intensity

The same contrast seen in so many animal species appears also in literally all cultures across the face of the earth. Why so?

The broadly accepted explanation was found by biologists George Williams and Robert Trivers just over a generation ago.[11] Since a female invests more in each offspring, she does well to choose carefully, looking for optimum advantage in each mating. By contrast, a promiscuous male who can sow his seed far and wide gains a significant genetic footprint in the next generation.[12] The key factor here is "parental investment," which is the amount a sex partner ordinarily invests in a youngster. Those who invest more in the offspring ordinarily do best to select carefully, to get the most from their investment, while those who invest little will profit from being sexual opportunists. Females ordinarily invest more in offspring—in our own species and in almost all of the other species as well.

In the rare exceptions, including sea snipes, Emperor Penguins, and sea horses, the males invest by incubating the eggs.[13] In these unusual arrangements, the females court potential mates as much as the other way around. These extraordinary exceptions prove the rule, with those who invest more being choosier.[14]

Contrasts in sexual intensity correspond roughly to the contrasts in parental investment. Investment in youngsters is surely more similar among humans than among many mammals, with men generally supporting their women and their biological children. And the sexual interest is surely more similar among our own than among familiar animals such as dogs or horses, where the males contribute the sperm and little else.

Among humans, social obligation strongly affects the balance in sexual interest. In the University of Hawaii study, the strictly casual situation suggests that the young man would have no commitment at all and that the young woman would deal with the consequences on her own. We saw an almost complete separation in sexual willingness, with three quarters of the boys going for the deal and virtually none of the girls. In an ordinary courtship or in a marriage, a recognized relationship suggests that the man should and probably will invest in the parenting, and in recognized relationships the levels of interest between men and women converge so that it is only moderately out of balance.

It has been argued that males are more interested in sex because cultures are stricter with females and strongly inhibit their sexuality. Yet Western culture today is relatively permissive with females, allowing young women considerable leeway to participate in sex or not as they wish. Yet men continue to pursue and women still expect to be courted. The better explanation is the one that applies as broadly as possible not just to one situation or another but for all species, all cultures, all eras and all circumstances, anywhere observed.

Natural selection proceeds through the survival of the fittest, as those best adapted to their situations survive to produce youngsters with similar adaptive qualities.[15] In addition to surviving, we must mate and pair our own genes with those from the opposite sex to produce offspring. So evolution proceeds also through the selection of sex partners who provide the other half of the genetic requirements. What we refer to as "sexual selection" or as "mate selection" contributes significantly to many of our gender-typical traits.[16]

Onboard passions among civilized humans

Men are from Mars and women are from Venus, according to a popular title by John Gray.[17] It is an appealing metaphor. Given all the misunderstandings between us, we might as well be from separate planets. Why are we so far apart? We are all from Earth, obviously, but we are not from the same stations on Earth. We come from the same geographic locations, but we have not faced the same social and biological requirements. Since earliest times, according to anthropologists, men and women have always performed separate tasks, living complementary but essentially parallel lives. Life in the male stations and life in the female stations required from us different qualities for our respective survival and procreation. Why should it surprise anyone that we might evolve not just different anatomies, but different psychologies as well?

> Men are from earth.
> Women are from earth.
> Deal with it!
>
> —cartoonist Art Bouthillier

Solid sex differences are being found in how our brains process information and emotions.[18] Women typically process emotional concerns in both hemispheres of the brain and exchange information more easily between hemispheres, while men process emotional concerns mainly in the right side and reserve the left side for language and reasoning. Our contrasting brain processes clearly contribute to our contrasting emotional temperaments. The advantages, suggests *Brain Sex* author Anne Moir, are that women are more adept at expressing emotions, as we observe, while men more clearly separate reasoning from emotions.[19] Magnetic imaging that can now map our brain activity shows again and again that male and female brains operate differently.

Our genes are found to contribute to a wide range of features, from the trivial through the most important and fundamental. Even basic happiness is easier for those with optimistic genes. *Authentic Happiness* author Martin Seligman estimates that fully half of the variations in happiness are genetic, while about an eighth is due to circumstances and the remaining three-eights can be brought under personal control.[20]

Which is more important, our socialization or our genes? Columnist Marilyn vos Savant quips that your genes are obviously more fundamental, as they say whether you are a banana, a butterfly, or a human being. Fair enough.

Among humans, which is more important? Within a recognizable society such as America, analysis suggests that between 30 and 50% of the variations between individuals in personality and temperament is inborn.[21] Such figures are calculated mainly from twin studies, where identical twins reared apart are found to have quite similar temperaments, while two unrelated youngsters reared in the same family show relatively few similarities. Thus 30–50% of what makes you different and unique seems to be a result of the genetic blueprints you inherited from your line of ancestors. Society molds and shapes us, of course, but we must already have the stuff to be molded and shaped. Inside us somewhere are the emotions, appetites and passions—the "oomph," if you will, the vital juices—that incline us to fit in and adapt to what society expects of us.

An extensive review in the *American Psychologist* concludes that across cultures, human evolution accounts for the overall pattern of gender differences much better than strictly social explanations.[22] While any single evolutionary explanation can be questioned, the full pattern of explanations is highly convincing.

We present here a few such explanations, for your consideration. See these not as proven truths, but as plausible accounts. Reserve judgment. Wait until you see the entire pattern, and then make up your own mind. See evolution, if you wish, as a fascinating way to organize the information and remember it. At the least, it will help lock in your mind some of the patterns of gender conflict that so affect our lives.

The gist of natural selection is straightforward: Genetic variations contribute to variations in traits, and the more adaptive variations survive and flourish and so gradually replace the less adaptive ones.[23] It is perhaps surprising that such a simple principle should have such profound implications.

For those doing the arithmetic, the 30–50% of individual qualities accounted for by our genes still leaves fully 50–70% to be accounted for by various social factors. Our emphasis on innate tendencies here is merely meant to provide balance, as these have been so often ignored in mainstream writing.

Of course, nature and nurture must work together. Consider the language we speak, which is a matter of culture. The French speak French, the English speak English, we all speak what we hear, and so it goes. Yet all human societies use some language, anywhere in the world. So it is right to say that the use of language is human nature. The view that lower animals act on instinct but humans are free of such things is far too simplistic. A human toddler assimilates language with or without social prompting, indicating an innate language instinct at least as complex as anything found in any of the animal species.[24]

Culture refers to the differences between communities, whereas human nature refers to the commonalities between individuals, across cultures. Culture and human nature combine to produce our actual gender differences.

Men and women do indeed want different things from each other. Consider the sexes as if we were separate species, suggests biologist Robert Trivers, where your opposite is a principal resource for producing offspring.[25] It sometimes seems like men and women are designed to make each other miserable, which is not the case. Men and women are designed to use one another for our own reproductive advantage, and in doing so we just happen to make each other miserable. Yet it would seem that we could find enough in common to maintain the many advantages of committed partnerships.

Human nature suggests solutions

We will look at how nature draws our conscious minds into its service. Sex, for instance, is a genetically engineered program for creating a viable copy of half of our genes. This does not mean that we ordinarily have sex in order to replicate our genes. Typically, we have sex simply because we want to and we *feel* like it. Exactly! Nature programs into our conscious minds the feelings and the will to do what has promoted our genes. Biological mechanisms trigger conscious yearnings, and we act on our yearnings without ever considering what nature accomplishes through our actions.

Seeing how nature uses sex to reproduce allows us to seize control of our destinies. By using our wits and medical technology, we can find a half dozen ways to circumvent its natural mechanisms. So too with our innate emotional programming. Understanding how nature programs our minds invites us to step back and smile at ourselves and to adjust our reactions to better suit our more noble purposes.

Some object to biological explanations, fearing that it means limits on free will. If gender qualities are somewhat innate, then we are not free to be anything and everything we might wish to be. We see such explanation not as constraining us, but as helping to set us free. You do not master human nature by ignoring it or imagining you are too far above it to concern yourself with it. We become wiser, stronger, and more compassionate as we come to understand human nature and learn to work within it and work around it. Understanding human nature can open your eyes, expand your choices, and free you from the biological machinery that you never realized was moving you in the first place.

Our biological nature has served us well over the eons, contributing to the survival of the human species. And in many cases, our automatic and emotional responses still serve us well. Fear, which impelled us to flee lions and to be suspicious of outsiders, now pressures us to study for tests and to prepare for a cold and unknown future.[26] The apprehension that many of us live with is a remnant of our adaptive mechanisms.

Our natural reactions may be in the best interests of our genes, but not in our best interests personally. Shame and guilt pressure individuals to conform to group expectations, and so inhibit reckless transgressions and maintain socially proper conduct. Yet, these emotions can be truly painful.

Innate tendencies can be changed, of course, although not by merely wishing them away. Change requires conscientious attention and goes slowly. And to change anything, we must begin where we actually are and not where we wish we were or where we think we should be.

Ideology vs. Observation

We have presented the University of Hawaii findings to several graduate psychology classes, wherein students invariably quarrel with the results. The students suggest the experiment was improperly conducted and not credible, and argue strongly that men and women are not that different.

So we ask the young men if they would go for casual sex in such circumstances. The guys laugh, joke, and tacitly acknowledge that yes, they would go for it. When we ask the young women, they feel the whole arrangement was most improper and insulting to women and that obviously no, they would not accept it. So among these bright young adults who could hardly accept that men and women could be so far apart, each would personally acknowledge that he or she would react just as the University of Hawaii students did. The University of Hawaii study has been replicated several times, always with the same results.

As in so many masquerades, ideology trumps observation. These highly intelligent students believed the ideology of their instructors, as was expected of them, that men and women are essentially the same, when even a simple review of their own experiences could have told them that it was patently not so.

Cookie-cutter ideology

Males are biologically more inclined to casual sex than females, among humans across the face of the globe and across mating species anywhere in the world. The finding is obvious enough.. But being obvious does not mean that it is necessarily proper or acceptable to state it openly.

A prevalent ideology holds that all groups must be equal, for justice to prevail. So therefore, we must be all the same, in intelligence and temperament and talents and anything else that might contribute to inequalities. The ideologues contend that our genetics must not, and therefore cannot and do not contribute anything at all to our temperaments. The true believers here are adamant and quite intolerant of those who conclude otherwise.

Yet we are not all Silly Putty, ready to be molded into anything the social idealists wish us to be. Once we acknowledge that nature contributes to even a single important trait such as sexual interest, then we are on a slippery slope and may lose faith, sliding too easily into the obvious realization that our genetic legacies contribute to a wide variety of features. Once we accept that men and women are innately different in casual lust, then it is easier to consider that we can have innate differences in other qualities as well.

So, to promote a plain vanilla vision of equality, the social purist wants to mask over our innate qualities and pretend that all human groups are inherently the same. While the idealism may appear noble, the insistent pretender is hardly a wise guide amid unfamiliar and sometimes perilous territory.

Surely nature has not stamped men and women out as cookie-cutter copies of each other. We would do well to accept that individuals are given unique gifts and talents along with personal weaknesses and vices as well.

The ideology itself is merely a social convention, of course. A century ago, and through hundreds of thousands of years of human existence, while we lived close to nature and observed, everyone knew that young males are simply steamier.

Flesh and spirit

Some object to biological parallels on religious grounds. Yet Judeo-Christian traditions see human nature as "flesh" and "spirit," meaning biological and also spiritual. The late Pope John Paul II acknowledged that the science of human evolution is probably so, along with the Big Bang, and then went on to reconfirm that however the world was created, God was there.[27] In an official statement, the National Association of Biology Teachers no longer insists that the mutations behind evolution must be random ones, correctly realizing that science cannot categorize these unobserved changes as either strictly random or unfolding by some unseen plan. The Buddhist and Hindu quests for higher spiritual consciousness recognize that we must wrestle with the "monkey brain" or "monkey mind" within, referring to our biological natures. So we see here that religion and science need not continue to lock horns at all, but can find ways to accommodate each other.

The challenge is to accept our natures, to understand them and take them into account, and to work with them or work around them to fashion functional relations that are truly fair and equal and not just pleasant masquerades that cover up festering incompatibilities.

Men Compensate Women

Most adamantly, the finding that men have higher sexual interest does not mean that men have sex more with women than women have with men. Obviously, anytime a man has sex with a woman, that woman is also having sex with that man. So logically, men and women must have sex with each other at the same times, in the same places, with the same average frequency, and with the same number of partners. The logic holds anywhere where the numbers of men and women in the population are approximately the same.

Early surveys reporting that men begin sexual relations younger than women and are more sexually active are skewed by sampling errors or responder biases.[28] Both sexes tend to fudge a bit in the socially desirable direction. Men overestimate, to appear more successful, and women underestimate, to appear more modest and virtuous.

The common presumption that men have sex more frequently and with more partners than women is another colorful feature of the social masquerade. Impossible by simple logic, it reflects who we pretend to be and not who we actually are.

The higher male sex drive does mean that men must typically court women and meet their expectations, to gain access, and that women can ordinarily expect some compensation for their sexual favors.

The custom seems to be a human universal. Anthropologist Bronislaw Malinowski observed sexual practices among the uninhibited Trobriand Islanders, who were separated from other cultures for tens of thousands of years. "In the course of every love affair," he notes, "the man has constantly to give small presents to the woman. To the natives, the need of one-sided payment is self-evident. The custom implies that sexual intercourse, even where there is mutual attachment, is a service rendered by the female to the male."[29]

So too in cultures around the world. A woman in a primitive Kung San[30] hunter-gatherer village tells of the benefits of affairs: "When you have lovers, one brings you something and another brings you something else. One comes at night with meat, another with money, another with beads. Your husband also does things and gives them to you."[31] Indeed, around the world, men are observed to give women tasty treats and various presents as a prelude to lovemaking.[32] In foraging societies, women openly demand gifts from their lovers, usually in the form of protein-rich meat. "If men want sex for its own sake," notes Harvard psychologist Steven Pinker, "women can make them pay for it."[33]

The practice also extends back to our closest primate cousins. A female bonobo, or pygmy chimp, is often willing to provide sex in exchange for a fruit or a hunk of meat, which she eats and satisfies herself while he satisfies himself with her. By our human standards, it seems humiliating to the male for his mate to snack while he copulates with her. Yet the female seems quite content with the eats and the male seems not to mind at all. Among chimpanzees, a male is more likely to give meat to a female when she is fertile. Indeed, when chimpanzees divide up a kill, the receptive estrous females get a larger share of meat.[34]

Some insects show similar behavior. Among hanging flies, the male catches prey and offers it to the female, who allows him to mount her while she eats it. The larger the offering, the longer she allows him to ride.[35] So compensated sex surely qualifies as one of the oldest professions on Earth, commonly practiced among various animal species many millions of years before the arrival of Homo sapiens.

> By the age old contract,
> young women will trade sex for anything they want,
> while men will trade anything they have for sex.
>
> — Columnist Fred Reed

Fast forward to the here and now: Among men and women dining out together in elegant restaurants, the man pays the tab about ten times to every one time a woman pays.[36] A man who courts generally pays for the meals and entertainment, implicitly compensating the woman not just for the privilege of her company but also for the possibility of sexual favors afterward.

Among lower animals, the compensation can be immediate and edible, although a female may also select for superior genes or to gain protection for her offspring and the benefits of friendship. Among men and women, compensation is more complex and usually more implicit.

Above all else, the masquerade requires that the exchange remain unspoken. An interested man may properly give a woman any of a variety of gifts and favors but not cash, at least not initially, as cash suggests a commercial relationship with no further obligations. The gifts are supposed to be seen as symbols of a commitment indicating love and respect, the willingness to provide, and the resources to do so. A woman who gains a committed man who supports her and her children does better than one who gains only an evening of drinks and flattery.

So how much should a woman expect from a man, and how much is he obligated to provide for her? Our emotional reactions run high. A man should surely respect the woman, consider her feelings, accept her as she is and not quarrel with her too much, commit to her after an appropriate time and not string her along, and support any children which might result. We seem to know what is honorable and fair, and we object to men using women. And while we know that women should expect something, which is only proper, we also know that it is not and cannot be called compensation for sexual favors, which is too similar to prostitution, which is absolutely improper. So simple social propriety prevents us from mentioning the obvious.

Women are more sought after as sex partners than are men. So in the coarse terms of free market economics, as much as we want to avoid the obvious, sex with young women is simply more valuable than is sex with young men. Those who possess the more valuable commodity can require compensation for it, while those who want the valuable commodity can be required to provide that compensation. Just how and why women are compensated sneaks its way into important facets of our most intimate relationships. We look at the particulars of how we arrange proper compensation.

CR   SO

2.

Emotional Firepower

Conflict is a growth industry.

— Roger Fisher and William Ury

If half of a good marriage is in the ways we understand and enjoy each other, the other half rests upon how well we slide through everyday conflict when it occurs and stay on course and remain friends.[1]

Equality

Given the importance we place on equality, we might expect that relationships would be best in which men and women listen to each other and have about equal say in joint decisions. And that is exactly what the research shows. Marriages in which husbands and wives participate together and share power about equally are found to be more satisfying[2] and more stable. In the realm of relationships, as in the broader society, equality has practical benefits.

How close are marriages to our egalitarian ideals? We look here at how men and women typically share power in Western relationships. Be prepared for some surprises.

Most arguments are about who is being mistreated and cheated and who is taking unfair advantage. Yet we will see here that gender relationships are governed as much by our primal passions as by any abstract standards of fairness. Indeed, the fairness standard seems to be a ruse, a window dressing, to cover our most primal convictions and make them sound proper.

While men are more intrigued by sexual relations, women want to make sure they are benefiting from a relationship and not being used. We see how this plays out in everyday arguments.

Candid Observations

In government and industry, men hold the major positions of power. But how does power in the public and business realms translate into power in personal relationships? To find out, we eavesdrop on a seemingly typical couple, in the midst of one of their typical arguments.

"All you care about is work and sports," Melissa accuses. "You are never willing to go anywhere with just me, without the children along. I'm just a convenience to you. I cook the meals. I clean the house. I'm here for sex. You take it all for granted!"

In return, Jason says, well... nothing! She waits. "What do you want me to say?" he finally mutters, vaguely, not really addressing the accusation. She feels he is evading her questions; he feels invaded by her questioning.

So what is going on here? Why is she the one doing the arguing, and why is he not arguing back? Is this a typical pattern, or are such highly argumentative women somewhat unusual? Is this an unusual man, or are most men similarly passive in the face of female anger?

Jason is what used to be called the strong, silent type. But is he as calm as he appears? Is he so far above her that he can simply snooze through her criticism and not even bother to answer her complaints? Or is it just the opposite? Is he too confused and too overwhelmed by her anger to argue successfully against her? Is he simply enduring until she gets over it because he is too intimidated to do much of anything else? How can we tell?

Fortunately, social scientists are voyeurs. Researchers observe closely, trying to see us as we really are—and not as we try to present ourselves or as society expects us to be. Observation has a nonchalant way of contradicting our folklore and offending our sense of how things ought to be.

Eavesdropping

Researcher John Gottman at the University of Washington has a laboratory set up to observe and measure what goes on when couples argue. He invites couples into his lab, where he records their pulse rates, heart output, skin conductance, and other indicators of stress. A video camera records their conversation as well as facial expressions and mannerisms such as fidgeting.

Gottman does not ask couples to fight, which would be improper. Instead, he helps couples identify a major area of disagreement, and then he asks them to discuss the issues and try to reach a resolution. And of course, they fight.

Women are more confrontive

Gottman observes that women are freer and more open in expressing their anger than are men. Wives introduce complaints more than husbands, bringing concerns to the surface. Once arguing, wives tend to further justify their positions and introduce additional complaints, thus expanding arguments, while husbands try to contain the argument.[3]

The finding that women are more argumentative is substantial and robust, and has been observed by numerous other researchers as well.[4] It is seen among couples of high and low social and economic status and those in the middle.[5] It is found by direct observation[6] and from reports from the couples themselves.[7] Men report that their wives argue more, and women report that their husbands tend to withdraw. And such imbalanced confrontation is not merely a product of our current era. Early social sciences research in the mid 1930s showed a similar pattern, with women typically pursuing arguments and men withdrawing.[8]

The imbalance is also obvious to any therapist who observes even a few marriages.[9] At a presentation at our state association, we asked my fellow psychologists, "Who is more open and forceful in their complaints against their mates, men or women?"[10] Of the forty psychologists present, all but a couple raised their hands to indicate that the wives complain more than the husbands. None claimed to have observed the opposite.

How strong are the findings? Women dominate in marital arguments about twice as often as men dominate. In the most lopsided arguments, one partner argues while the other maintains silence, waiting for it to be over. Would it surprise you that of those silent in marital arguments, 85% are men and only 15% women?[11] So, in those single participant arguments, by a ratio of six to one, it is the women who complain and accuse and the men who are being accused. Gender casts individuals as argumentative or passive in these most severe marital squalls, more so than any other characteristic or all of them put together.[12] The observed six to one ratio is absurdly high.

In these select situations, it is as if men and women are no longer made up of the same stuffing. As in strictly casual sex, we see here in serious confrontations an almost complete separation between the men and the women.

In our talks, we survey our audiences. We ask, "When you were a youngster, was it your mom or your dad who typically argued harder and got his or her way?" We ask, "In your own relationships, who argues harder and usually gets his or her way?" The men and women report about the same things. It was the mothers who usually argued more than the fathers, and the women today who argue more strongly than the men.

We found only a single exception, in a group of college honors psychology students, mainly female, who indicated that their parents shared the air time about equally. These highly functional young women appear to be the products of highly egalitarian marriages. Yet when asked who dominated in their own relationships, twelve of the fourteen girls indicated that they dominated, and the two boys in the class indicated that they found their girlfriends overbearing. Whatever benefits these exceptional youngsters gained from their own egalitarian parents is not apt to be passed along to their own children.

Argument has an upside as well as the obvious unpleasantries. A confrontation can establish a connection or express a problem, and women who argue usually see themselves as facing important concerns while their husbands try to avoid them. Confrontation is a way of expressing grievances, and those who do so usually consider themselves quite justified.

Men are more stressed by conflict

Gottman finds that men tend to be more stressed by marital arguments, compared to women, who are more comfortable with emotional confrontation and better at it.[13] Similarly, Robert Levenson at the University of California at Berkley finds that husbands uniformly find quarrels unpleasant and often overwhelming, whereas many of the wives do not mind so much.[14] As absurd as it may sound, the typical man is more stressed when his wife is upset than is the wife herself.

Most men show stress as soon as an argument begins. Average resting heart rate is about 72 for men and 82 for women. As his wife complains to her husband that he never listens, on the very next beat his heart rate can be up and racing at ten or twenty or even as many as thirty beats per second faster than the moment before.[15] Obviously, men are readily overwhelmed and flooded when their mates are irritated. In his look at male reactivity, emotional intelligence author Daniel Goleman suggests men are "hijacked" by their own emotional over-arousal.[16]

Stress goes down somewhat for men who stop talking altogether, suggesting that silence serves as sanctuary to protect against overwhelming emotion. Unfortunately, as the man stops talking, his wife's stress increases.

In slightly different terms, men are more easily overwhelmed by emotional conflict than are women, reacting more strongly to less provocation. A typical man is seriously troubled whenever his wife criticizes him, while a woman can usually handle criticism unless her mate becomes truly contemptuous.[17] Contrary to popular expectations, men are markedly more intimidated by angry women than women are by angry men. Men tend to become confused during such confrontations, more so than women, losing track of what is said and where the argument is going. Men are not ordinarily blindfolded or gagged in arguments with women—it just seems that way. Overwhelmed by female anger, men fold.

How do men explain why they often withdraw from their wives rather than arguing hard for a win? A man might say that he wants to do "what's right," or he does not want to "get the wife upset." He might say, "It is no use arguing with her because it just makes her mad."

Men typically *appear* calmer than their wives, who are more visibly upset, so it is easy to be fooled. Remember that the appearance is merely a masquerade. A typical man whose wife is upset with him is highly stressed by it, regardless of how unruffled he manages to appear.

The silence is often referred to as "stonewalling," and it does lower stress for men and thwart their wives. Yet crouching behind a stone wall remains a tactic of those who have no voice and lack the will to confront the argument head on. It is also an "I'll take my marbles and go home" tactic, as one bails out of the conversation and wanders into social and emotional isolation.

Men remain bitter afterward

After a caustic exchange, stress falls off more rapidly for women while it remains higher for men. Women recover more quickly after an argument, while men tend to rehash it in their minds and continue to feel trashed and bitter about it.[18] Men are more apt to be hurt hours, days, or even weeks after an argument.

As odd as it might seem, those who experience more bitterness after arguments are not necessarily more inclined to initiate further argument. Women recover more quickly from a confrontation and then are more willing to initiate the next round, while men feel trashed and bitter longer afterward and so want to let it go, forget it, and avoid further confrontations.

In brief

Women are seen to be more willing to initiate conflict, more willing to escalate conflict, better able to handle it when it occurs, and quicker to recover from it.[19] Men, in contrast, seek to avoid conflict, try to contain it when it occurs, are less competent in handling conflict, and take longer to recover from it. Women are generally more comfortable with relationship conflict and are more verbally confrontive while men, who are more stressed by it, tend to placate, concede, or withdraw.

So the typical man who says little or nothing in an argument is surely not as totally above it all as he might appear. He is stressed to his eyebrows and hardly able to argue successfully against his more verbally confrontive wife.

> In the sea of conflict, men sink and women swim.
>
> — John Gottman

The observation that women tend to be more argumentive should surely not be misunderstood to mean that women are more argumentive in all relationships or in all instances. Women dominate in about two out of three marital arguments, meaning that men dominate in about one out of three. We focus here on how and why women argue while men withdraw, because that is the more normal and typical pattern in relationships. If that is not the pattern in your own relationship, then the material presented here does not apply to you, or it applies in reverse. Compare your own relationship to the typical pattern, identify how you are similar or not the same at all, and see what you can learn from it.

Implications

Women consume about 85% of the relationship literature, while men read a paltry 15% of it. Would it be too obvious to suggest that we need to understand men better and to guide and support and coax men to be more active participants in relationships? Programs to engage men will surely benefit the women as well.

So far as we have little or no real power and no chance of gaining any, then that is truly tragic. So far as we have power but are too caught up in ourselves to take advantage of it, then that might be considered simple folly. We will look at ways men and women might better use the opportunities open to them.

We might mention the obvious, that dominating in an argument does not necessarily get you what you want and can prove worthless or even backfire. We will look further at how arguments manage and mismanage our relationships.

Women wonder if men who withdraw in arguments are weak and inadequate, or simply unconcerned and withholding. Yet the most normal and typical men are truly uncomfortable with upset women, and therein lies the answer.

> You should recognize that most men do not and cannot argue with upset women. Realize that a man who avoids arguing with you is not showing himself to be unusually weak or blissfully unconcerned. He is just being a normal man. It's a guy thing.

Women can be quite unaware of how much power their anger actually has over men. Of course, it is natural in the midst of an argument to focus only on our own grievances and to overlook how much we are battering our adversaries. And this may be especially easy for women, since men often *appear* calmer in arguments and do not show themselves to be as stressed and upset as women do.

> You might realize that men are more vulnerable in conflict than they appear and slower to recover from it. Be careful to accurately gauge how much stress your accusations inflict, and make allowances. Even a little anger can have more than the intended effect.

Perhaps women in earlier generations were more aware of male vulnerability. Men were said to have "big egos" or "fragile egos." Both expressions, it seems, refer to men being more readily hurt when accused, criticized, or simply ignored. Daughters were taught to be aware of this and advised to deal with men carefully. Women today figure that men should not be the way they are and ought to straighten up, which is grand in its idealism but hardly practical. Managing a relationship requires making real allowances for real limitations.

♂ To better resolve conflict, you must learn to be more comfortable with it. What does it take to shrug off a critical comment instead of coming totally unraveled over it? Recognize that it is normal for women to be more easily upset and irritated than men, but that women also get over it faster. Do not interpret it as a great catastrophe when your mate is bothered about something. Try to mentally separate yourself from the heat of an argument, and remain as calm as possible. Stay involved, and try to talk it out.

In earlier generations, men considered women overly emotional and often unfathomable. To some extent, that attitude helped men contend with women by not taking it so deathly seriously when women were upset. Men were to uphold their responsibilities and not worry too much about emotions they could not control. Today, we are not supposed to mention that women can be highly emotional. Our politically correct blinders obscure our vision and limit our ability to deal with relationships. Caught by surprise when the sweet wife turns moody or hostile, men take it far too personally.

♂ Recognize that women are now and always have been more comfortable with anger and other emotions. The obvious solution is to settle in and adjust to it.

Even excellent relationships have misunderstandings, colliding interests, and occasional confrontations. John Gottman concludes that it is not necessarily the conflict which causes ill will, but rather the inability to repair the breach and continue on. "What matters most is the ability to repair things when they go wrong."[20]

Remember that men are more apt to feel trashed and bitter long after a confrontation.

Find a way to resolve your sense of injury and to re-involve yourself. You might tell your wife that you feel wrecked by the confrontation, and ask her to give you some time to pull yourself together. Tell her that you will get back with her as soon as you can sort it out. You thus acknowledge you are overwhelmed, which she may not have realized, and you commit yourself to repairing the rift and remaining involved. It is easy to be blown away in an argument, but nursing your personal wounds afterward is not going to make anything better.

The woman who argues while her husband is speechless feels justified: After all, he is the one causing the problem by sitting on his feelings and not communicating with her. The man who withdraws feels justified too: She is the one who flies at him over anything, smashes him before he knows what is happening, and then expects him to open up and communicate with her.

While women are typically more confrontive, the positions are often reversed. Either way, the one who gets the best in the outburst feels it ought to end there, while the one who feels beaten up remains wary.

 If you see yourself in this pattern, realize there is nothing superior about either open anger or mistrust and withdrawal. Think about changing yourself.

In the midst of an angry barrage, those who scold feel mistreated and justified and oh so righteous in their causes, while those who are being scolded feel mistreated as well but also disrespected, ashamed, and inadequate. Is it not odd that human nature might incline us toward such serious quarrels?

Remember that anger and wisdom are strange bedfellows. Besting your opposite does not make your argument true or just, nor does being bested make you wrong or unfair. And each of your imbalanced arguments tends to produce continuing unpleasantries.

Taken for Granted

The advantages of women saying what they want and expressing their feelings show up in marriage research. Some patterns of marital conflict are beneficial in the long run, concludes John Gottman, even if they are unsettling at the time. The woman who is always agreeable and compliant often finds that her marriage deteriorates over time.[21]

What is it about the understanding, compliant woman that should cause a relationship to unravel? Is the sweet, generous woman not just what any man could possibly want?

Some of these uncomplaining women are annoyed inside but unwilling to say anything, and you can understand why they have poor marriages. But others are truly pleasers—straightforwardly interested in making a man happy and not wanting to see him upset or annoyed. Their misfortunes seem most undeserved.

An early look at blue-collar relationships found that the working men say they want a woman who will come over to the house, watch the game and drink beer with the buddies, prepare a meal, and stay over for the night. She sounds like a pleasant enough ideal, but here is the surprise: These same men tend to drift away from their pleasant companions and marry the women who demand to be taken out and treated with more respect.[22]

We have seen the pattern play out again and again. We talk to personable men who have had a number of satisfactory relationships with pleasant women, all of which ended amicably, and now find themselves married to a dragon who carps at every trivial offense. The pleasant women did not hold on and were willing to let the fellow go along on his way, if that is what he wanted, while the tougher woman who finally caught the fellow had what we might call "claws." She was offended when he hinted at separating, and she refused to go along with it. She scolded him and accused him of running a line on her when he said he loved her. She accused him of just using her. To convince her and perhaps himself that he was not the user he appeared to be, he had to stay and talk it out with her. And so he stayed.

We also talk to some of the sweetest and most nurturing women who are married to grouchy men who are oblivious to the courtesies and blame their wives for every minor inconvenience. The more she understands his complaints, the more he indulges himself in them until his complaints seem to own him. These men take the understanding for granted and seem to have not the vaguest idea how life plays out in the more typical households.

It is easy to idealize the warm, compliant woman who accepts a man and goes along with anything he wants, but the average man will hardly be in awe of her and will soon take her for granted. A wife usually exerts a fair amount of control in a marriage, and a woman who goes along with anything and everything her husband wants is acting more like a servant or a slave than like a wife. Remember that in our formative years, most cultures allowed polygamy even though few men had the resources to support a second wife. A woman who is always contented with her man allows him to feel he is doing so well that he could maybe have room for another woman in his life.

In contrast, women who stand up for themselves command respect and compliance, and the same men who resent being scolded nonetheless respect the power and are swayed by the intense emotional involvement.

All this may be a surprise, but it should not be. Why would so many women be so much more argumentive than men, were it not in their genetic interests? Nature is not benign, but neither is it intentionally malicious. It did not give women an extra helping of pushiness just to cause some poor slob grief. Nature balances argument with compliance and cooperation in proportion to how they have benefited our genes.

Our hearts go out to these especially nurturing women. Some hard advice, however, will be more useful:

 Toughen up and expect something more from your man. By standing up for yourself, you ask to be taken seriously. Involve your husband in your feelings and concerns, and you strengthen the bond between you. The art is in being insistent enough to be in his heart and mind, but not so over-bearing that you wreck everything while you are there.

♂ Our advice to men with especially nurturing women is to recognize what a totally sweet deal you have, and to realize that the next woman might not be so pleasant. Realize that many men are programmed to take advantage of the especially generous woman, and that you may be so pro-grammed as well. Monitor yourself, strengthen your commit-ment, and count your blessings.

How do we reconcile being generous and understanding with being tough enough to command respect and be treated well? The challenge is to observe closely and to gauge carefully how much toughness is required and how much tenderness will be repaid in kind. It is not an easy undertaking, but it yields serious advantages and there is no simpler way to figure out the right thing to do.

Men with pushy women grow weary of being bossed around and firmly believe that they would have a better relationship with a more agreeable companion. The illusion for many of these men is that a compliant woman is the source of happiness and that they would really appreciate the woman who gives in and goes along with what-ever they want. While the average man cannot appreciate it when his wife demands her way or gripes at him, a typical relationship may be better off for it in the long run, and he may be better off for it as well.

♂ You might see if you can understand as many of the complaints and criticisms as possible, realizing that these fractious interludes are but normal facets of typical marriages and that surely some of them are reasonable and just. Consider how you can meet legitimate concerns and can soothe hurt feelings.

How much pressure should women put on men to ensure commitment and support? We see here that overly compliant women fail to command respect, and that insistence in some matters typically improves a marriage. So while unrelenting complaints are indeed wearisome, the woman who can push for what she wants can help stabilize a marriage, so long as it is not overdone.

Origins

Women dominate in marital arguments in America, and probably in other similar Western societies as well. And it has been so as far back as the research can take us. As early as the Great Depression, through the total mobilization of World War II, the popularization of television and mass advertising, the comfortable fifties and rebellious sixties, through traditional marriages and dual career marriages, before feminism and on past it, and into the amorphous present, the findings are much the same: Women tend to voice their feelings in these highly personal arguments and men tend to withdraw.

In peasant societies where men monopolize all public positions of power, anthropologist Susan Rogers observes that women have a great deal of *informal* influence.[23] Indeed, neither men nor women in these communities believe that men actually rule women. Rogers concludes that men and women sustain a rough balance of power and that male dominance is a myth. Similarly, an analysis of almost a hundred pre-industrial societies concludes that women often exercise informal power well beyond what is afforded them by societal rules.[24] It would seem that the informal power that can tip personal arguments in favor of women is not a Western anomaly at all, but a common feature among many human societies.

We might imagine a culture somewhere which allows the most powerful men to issue orders but prohibits women from speaking back. Political arrangements which isolate women or prevent their participation have obvious impact. But we can still ask about human nature. In a relatively open culture such as ours, in which men and women can argue together, and in similar cultures around the world, why might human nature give women more voice in personal quarrels?

Mate selection (surprise!) seems to be the principal player.

Women choose

In selecting mates, women have some choice in almost all human communities. And so far as women have a choice, they will try to avoid those men who hurt or offend them or who cannot be counted upon to support their interests. The contentious young man who offends a young woman or refuses her requests will probably lose out to a man who does her favors and brings her gifts. So men who acquiesce to women or openly support them are more likely to mate and pass their genes along to the following generations. Concern for women can provide significant evolutionary advantage.[25]

Where marriages are arranged, as has often been the case, parents similarly favor the man who will support a daughter over one who might exploit and abandon her. Indeed, parents and family are often more concerned about such practical matters than the girls are themselves. An openly unsupportive man would be chosen last or probably not at all. Just as populations that support women are more successful, supportive men within those populations are also more successful in mating and passing their tendencies along to successive generations.

A prospective husband is judged not just on whether he was is to provide, but also on whether he is reliable and can be counted upon to do so. So the evolutionary consequences of insulting females or ignoring their concerns can be terribly severe. An average man who is too quick to oppose women has fewer children and so contributes fewer genes to the next generation.

Among our primitive ancestors, a girl was typically married by the time she reached fertility.[26] So her genetic interest was not simply to mate, which was the natural course, but to judge closely and to choose a man who might provide as well as possible for her and her children.

Among the various animal species, the higher sexual interest among males results in stronger competition between males and in females having a stronger hand in choosing their mates.[27] So far as females choose, the males must conform to the female standards.

Among frogs, the crooner who croaks the loudest wins fair damsel, whereas among birds, a male can score high by sporting the sharpest tail feathers. Most female birds find cleanliness attractive in a mate and find messy males unattractive. So too among humans. Whatever is required, males are inclined to oblige, and those who meet the standards pass their obliging genes into the next generation. The California fiddler crab may win top honors as the pickiest of species: On average, a typical female crab inspects over twenty male burrows before choosing the highest quality builder as her mate.[28]

Proper manners can be important in courtship. Among various birds, a female expects an interested male to show his intentions but then allow her to flit away and weigh her prospects before resuming the courtship. An overly aggressive suitor who is insensitive to her wishes will be rejected. Can we say that the courtship pattern bears an uncanny resemblance to human courtship?

Male southern right whales may be the best mannered suitors of all, for what is surely the oddest of reasons. A female southern right whale will mate with up to seven males, but only if they form an orderly queue.[29] So the males willingly line up and courteously await their turns, as the alternative is to lose out altogether.

How often do women choose men in our own society? Since men usually ask women out, are not the men making the choices? To find out, anthropologist David Givens and biologist Timothy Perper settled into singles hangouts and observed how men and women go about picking each other up.[30] Working separately, the two made remarkably similar observations. Women are seen to initiate about two-thirds of the courting sequences, inviting a man to approach by subtle cues such as a gaze or a smile. Women are quite aware of encouraging a man, by their attention, questions, compliments, and jokes, and by movements such as leaning unusually close or touching his arm. Later interviews revealed that most of the men see themselves as the initiators and are hardly aware that it is the woman who actually chooses her partner and then invites him into the chase.

Once the chase is on, it is typically the man who tries to persuade the woman to become sexually involved. He is the one who proposes a dinner or a show, who first reaches out to hold hands, who initiates the first kiss, who mentions going back to the apartment, who begins necking, and so on.[31] The woman then chooses to allow the man to go forward or to slow him down and wait to see how the relationship develops, or she opts out and looks for someone else. So after selecting the man who is to take her out, a woman then decides whether or not he gets lucky.

A beauty is a woman you notice; A charmer is one who notices you.

— Adlai Stevenson

Similar patterns are seen among high school students. If you want to know which boys will invite which girls to the prom, why interview the boys? Look at whom the girls gaze at and smile at and stand close to and giggle with. Boys approach girls who seem approachable and invite the girls who seem interested in being invited.

While most women understand the game, a few want to hover above it all and then wonder why men are not interested. A typical man will not ask a woman out unless she seems interested in being asked. He wants some assurance that he will be accepted before he puts his ego on the line.

Women choose in other cultures as well. While we think of men as the sexual initiators, women are seen to give the go ahead as much as men in 80% of almost a hundred societies surveyed.[32]

Charles Darwin observed that it is the female of the various species who ordinarily chooses her mate, more often than the males. While evolution has always been controversial, this particular observation so rankled the proper British gentlemen of his time that it was rejected outright, languishing for over a century before being finally resurrected and then solidly confirmed by modern investigators.

Curiously similar animals

Is it not odd indeed that one sex should so strongly dominate our political and public life while the opposite sex dominates in personal quarrels? Yet it is not a strictly human artifact—lower animals show similar arrangements.

Primatologist Frans de Waal notes that in greetings, the adult chimpanzee males are dominant and the chimpanzee females show deference 100% of the time.[33] In aggressive confrontations, the males win about 80% of the time. But in who takes food from whom, and who sits in the best spots, the females win about 80% of the time. That is, a female can usually take food away from a dominant male or nudge him aside to sit in the shade! So the males dominate when public status and rank are at stake, while females dominate in situations that concern their survival and personal comfort. How curiously similar to our human society! Would it surprise you that more than 98% of our human genetic blueprint is identical to that of chimpanzees?[34]

We find the same thing in other social mammals as well, which we explore later. Males tend to dominate in confrontations over status but often give way to females over scarce food. These odd reversals are closely tied to our sexual natures and our very different contributions to reproduction.

Acquiescence and sexual interest

Acquiescence may seem leagues away from sexual opportunism, but note that the two emerge from the same biological circumstances: Female reproduction involves a much higher investment than male reproduction, making the female reproductive resources scarcer and so comparatively more valuable. While female genes benefit from being more selective, male genes benefit from acquiescence and solicitous conduct, to gain access to the valuable female resources that transport them into the next generation.

Think of a young man who invites a young woman out to a posh restaurant and then to the theater, to impress her, and is attentive to her, flatters her, agrees with whatever she says, wanting to spend the night with her. He is doing what he figures she wants, voluntarily, supporting her opinions and even paying for the evening, in anticipation of snuggles later. If you have trouble seeing how male acquiescence and sexual opportunism fit together, look no further than your typical date.

Traits such as acquiescence to females and sexual opportunism can be only slightly advantageous and still prevail. So far as compliant men gain even a slight mating advantage in each generation, compliance would spread steadily through successive generations. Small advantages in each generation can add up to produce huge differences in innate traits. We have seen substantial gender differences in casual sex and in serious arguments.

Most of the sex differences we explore here are as obvious as these, and ratios of two to one or even more between men and women are common. Gender differences tend to be as large as findings in other areas of human behavior,[35] and those predicted from evolution tend to be especially large.[36]

Nature does not ordinarily program us by simple instinct, as occurs in lower animals. Rather our genes contribute to our interests and inclinations, which translate into actions. We have seen how human nature sets interest in casual sex higher in young men, but leaves women more inclined toward confrontations. Variations in socialization and personal experiences further adjust the settings, yielding an extraordinarily wide range of human inclinations.

Can We Accept Ourselves as We Are?

These observations are not at all flattering to men or to women. We want to see men as stronger and more independent than they appear here, and we want to see women as softer and gentler.

Men ordinarily hide their weaknesses and present themselves as in charge, wanting to seem strong even when they typically lose the arguments or withdraw to avoid losing. Indeed, women find it hard to respect men who fold in arguments. Men therefore benefit from their masquerade of strength and privilege and uphold it as best they can. Women who see themselves as mistreated underdogs fighting for a fair break, do not want to acknowledge that they usually out-argue their opposites in angry confrontations. Women want to believe that men have the real power and so ought to provide more. The ideology holds that since men are privileged and careless and since women are suppressed, women should feel more justified in unleashing the force of their anger against men. Anger, of course, is a primary weapon of emotional combat. The position justifies women and encourages them to express their anger, to support their grievances. Thus, women also benefit from their masquerade as soft and vulnerable, and take offense when it is challenged.

So as men and women, we collude to conceal how we actually are and to show ourselves instead as how we wish to be seen. We hide behind social masks and create agreeable myths about ourselves. And we are taken in by our own fabrications, mistaking our myths for reality. We *feel* that men are stronger, privileged, and in control of relationships, and we remember incidents that support our feelings but overlook those that do not. So here again, our masquerades prevail over simple realities.

Social etiquette also upholds the masquerade. We try to overlook it when a woman too openly dominates a man, as simple courtesy, so as not to embarrass her for being a dragon and him for being a milksop. In the splendid masquerade that is life, the men are strong while the women are sweet and nurturing. The actual incidents in which women boss men are hidden in the shadows, barely visible, and are ignored by everyone as much as is humanly possible.

Power

It has been argued that women dominate in arguments just to be heard, because men have the real power. That sounds almost right, and it surely sounds fair and practical. But it reverses the way real power works. The one who has the real power ordinarily dominates the arguments, not the subordinate. The boss can scold the gopher but not the other way around, as the boss runs the company and the gopher is expendable. And human nature has never been known to be particularly fair. Indeed, dominance in verbal confrontation is an obvious way of gaining power, holding power, showing power, and forwarding your own agenda. One who fails to hold his own either does not have the power or is fast on his way to losing it.

Most of us do not feel powerful in relationships, and we might presume therefore that our opposites must have the real power. It has been argued that the man whose wife is scolding him has the real power, as he is controlling her by not doing what she wants. Yet the man who is being scolded and not getting his way could hardly feel more powerful than the woman who is scolding him and not getting her way. All else being equal, would you not prefer to scold someone you are angry at rather than to take the scolding yourself?

Women argue strongly because they want to be heard and their husbands are not listening, which is understandable. Yet men also want to be understood, but fail to present a reasonable argument.

Social expectations provide not much of an explanation for why supposedly stronger men buckle in arguments with supposedly weaker women. It is as if the usual rules by which men ordinarily dominate are mysteriously suspended, and a new set of rules applies.

Power comes in many forms, of course. Men typically have more physical power than women, and the men who are in charge at work have more authority there, which is formal power. It is in the realm of personal arguments that women have the advantage. Women seem to have more of what we might call informal power or *emotional power*, which counts in personal relationships. We will look closely at how such power works.

The power of illusion

Professional masqueraders casually contradict the observables. "In contrast [to men]," according to *Dance of Anger* author Harriet Lerner, "women have been denied the forthright expression of even healthy and realistic anger."[37] And similarly, "Anger is an emotion that women express far less frequently than do men," according to Celia Halas. "In fact, men generally feel quite comfortable with anger, express it freely, and are reasonably careless about the problems it causes in other people. ... Women are generally afraid to express their anger."[38] These opinions are presented confidently but with nary a hint of supporting observation. The myth is repeated again and again until it morphs itself into the prevailing consensus.

The myth of careless men and restrained women is accepted not because it is observably so, but because it *feels* right. Perhaps nature is up to something here. Look at the above quotes and read between the lines: Since women are unfairly restrained and men are careless, women are justified therefore in unleashing the force of their anger against men, to support their grievances.

In any case, commentators who accept the commonplace myth that men dominate in personal relations go far amiss tracking the implications of an imaginary power imbalance. Only a few bother to observe personal arguments and report what they see.[39] Beginning as we do here with actual observations takes us on a controversial course through the uncharted territory behind the masquerades.

As marriage therapists, we are allowed to mention that this is the normal pattern and to help couples see how it explains their own interactions. Most men appreciate knowing that being confused in marital arguments is normal and not a shamefully unmasculine inadequacy. Many women appreciate knowing that the pattern is normal and then look for a practical way out of it.

To present the findings in public, it is best to poll the audience and then tally their observations. The audience volunteers the information and thus shares responsibility for it.

Forthright can be practical

I believe that the research findings are supportive of both men and women. Women show themselves not as weaklings, but as sturdy warriors of interpersonal conflict—comfortable with the give and take of the joust. Is that not more substantial than being the "weaker" sex? And while men are observed to be more stressed by conflict than we might expect, is it not more humane to recognize a limitation and make allowances for it, than to maintain unmanageable expectations? These findings are supportive of both sexes simply because they are true. Misunderstandings lead to unrealistic expectations, misguided actions, and failed relationships.

In so far as we want personally satisfying relationships based on reasonably equal voice in everyday decisions, we must chart our course carefully. If men were ordinarily more forceful in marital squabbles, then an increase in female power would promote equality. But since women are ordinarily more forceful, as observations indicate, the same solution pushes us farther apart. Men withdraw in the face of female accusation, leaving marriages emotionally barren and inhospitable. The challenge is to strike a proper balance, so that men and women can participate together and gain the best from each other.

After observing how men and women handled conflict, John Gottman looked in on his couples again three years later to see how they were faring. He found that the level of stress experienced in the earlier arguments, particularly by the husbands, clearly affected the future of their marriages. Those who were highly stressed tended to have deteriorating satisfaction over the next three years. Couples who could argue comfortably were more satisfied with their marriages over the same span. That much might be expected. It was the *strength* of the findings which is so glaring. Gottman found that the level of stress the men experience in conflict accounts for somewhat over 80% of the subsequent changes in marital satisfaction.[40] A connection this strong is quite unusual in social sciences research. The conclusion is clear: The man comfortable in conflicts with his wife is headed for a bright, rosy future, while high stress conflict means foul weather ahead and a possible shipwreck.

Why is the stress level among husbands so important? Men are more intimidated and more easily confused in angry confrontations, more apt to stonewall and withdraw into themselves, and more likely to feel trashed and bitter afterward. Amid the stresses and strains that conflict places upon relationships, men are the weaker link. Stress is obviously lower when men and women try to understand each other and particularly when we strive together to find that magic path to mutually satisfactory resolutions. So the stress a fellow experiences is both a problem in itself and also a particularly sensitive index of everything else going wrong in a relationship.

CR SO

Part II.
Chivalry Today

The rules of morality... are not conclusions of our reason.

— David Hume

Regardless of ideology or geography, affluence, race, creed, or color, or liberal or conservative philosophy, we can readily agree that men *ought* to support and protect women and not neglect women or allow them to be harmed. We so naturally expect that men should support women that it operates invisibly, in the background, as a standard for moral judgments.

"Chivalry" refers not just to the quaint customs of medieval knights or to the various superficial courtesies toward females. As used here, the term refers also to the inclination for men to support women, to champion their causes, to uphold their honor, and to protect them against other men who would harm them.

Some consider chivalry merely a flimsy folktale constructed to mask the subordination of women. Yet we can all identify striking instances where men and women alike appear to hold chivalrous standards, acting to support women and to hold men accountable.

CR ℘

3.

Chivalrous Passions

One of the most wickedly effective pick-up lines I have heard plays upon our chivalrous sympathies. A woman interested in a man walks up to him, takes his arm, and asks for his protection: "There's a fellow following me that I'm trying to lose. Would you be willing to act like you know me, and just talk to me for a few minutes, will you? I'd be ever so grateful." It seems to do the job just about every time. She casts her choice as a real man, protecting a woman who prefers him over another man. He feels like her champion and hero, and she takes it from there.

Note that the ruse would hardly work with the genders reversed. Imagine that a man interested in a woman walks up to her, takes her arm, and runs the same line: "There's a woman following me that I'm trying to lose. Act like you know me, and just talk to me for a few minutes, will you? I'd be ever so grateful." He thus casts himself as a lowly cad who gets involved with a woman and then tries to jilt her. Is he stringing her along? What a jerk! What woman would feel compelled to protect him from his callous irresponsibility?

A man who berates his wife is misusing his power. Most of us would judge him a bully and a tyrant, and we would want to stop him. Were we a father or brother, and not sensitive psychologists, we might take him aside, tell him that we expect him to straighten up, and let him know we mean business. Were we a mother or sister, we would voice our concerns and turn friends and family against him. We would all try to talk her into leaving him, and we would help her if she is willing to go.

Now switch it around. What about the woman who berates her husband? She makes us uncomfortable, surely, but we are not so sure about him, either. What did he do to make her so upset? Is he not treating her right? Anyway, what is he—a wuss? Real men are expected to take care of themselves and to take care of their wives as well. Is he not much of a man? How many of us would jump in on his side and argue his case against his upset wife? Not many, certainly. How many would try to get him to leave her? Again, not many.

See the contrast? We feel strongly that we ought to protect women from men who bully them, but we expect men to take care of themselves. We are morally outraged by men who are cruel to women, but we tend to stay out of it when women are harsh with men. Complaints that men mistreat women arouse our moral indignation, while complaints that women mistreat men seem to be mere whining.

Chivalrous Standards

We have seen that women berate their husbands almost twice as often as men berate their wives. We might properly say that men who scold women are insensitive bullies, whereas women who scold men are expressing their feelings, or that men who berate their wives are callous or cruel whereas women who berate their husbands are hurt or upset. Callous men should be held accountable, and often are, whereas upset women should be understood and assisted, and often are.

We are not impartial observers, but partisans in the great masquerade. We observe what is important to us, we talk about our concerns among family and friends, and we remember what suits our agendas. We are keenly aware of how men are in charge and how men mistreat women, while we hardly notice when it plays out the other way around. We are inclined to judge men as emotionally negligent or abusive and to see women as neglected and abused. Our moral and practical sensitivities focus on men mistreating women but then consign the reverse mistreatment to that shadowy underworld of pointless irrelevancies. Such contrasts are odd, but easily accepted because they are familiar and they reflect our sense of propriety and justice.

In a column on those awful parents who severely batter their children, conservative Christian family psychologist James Dobson refers to the perpetrators as malevolent men and disturbed women. To most of his readers, he seems to have it about right. We see men who batter children as sinister or evil, while we see women who do so as overwrought and dysfunctional.

Men and women each complain to their close friends, although women do considerably more of it. In the public realm we see a dramatic separation between the genders. Chivalrous standards accept women who complain about being mistreated and oppressed, although the tales of woe do get old. Yet only an extraordinarily foolish man would complain too publicly about being oppressed by women. He would reveal himself to be a loser and a weakling, and would garner contempt or pity but little support. Mistreated women ought to be allowed to express their justifiable complaints, while real men ought to accept their responsibilities toward women and not whine. Chivalrous standards concern us with only one side of the moral quandary, and leave us oblivious of the flip side.

Men ought to commit

Traditionally, in most cultures, a woman seeks a commitment in a love relationship, and her family and friends stand ready to help her. Emotions can run extremely high. Family and friends are outraged by the man who has sex with a woman but refuses to commit, and want him to either shoulder his responsibilities or be gone.

Family and friends can be more adamant than the woman is herself. Friends and relatives may try to convince her to leave the jerk, while she complains about him but stays because she has feelings for him. The woman who cannot get a commitment is being exploited, and if she willingly goes along with it she is allowing herself to be exploited. Note the asymmetry here. The man who cannot get a commitment from his lover is not a moral concern. We may feel sorry for him, but so what? We see males as sexually exploiting women and not the other way around, regardless of which partner refuses to commit. What sort of fool would try to get a man to leave a woman because he wants a permanent commitment and she will not give it?

Our sympathies go with upset women, who must be supported whenever children might be conceived. These same sympathies persist even when no children are expected, suggesting some assistance from our onboard inclinations.

Early Origins

A look at lower animals suggests that chivalrous sympathies come to us by way of our primate ancestors.

Amid famine

How do social animals apportion scarce resources? At Rutgers University, mixed-sex colonies of rats were underfed, then given food where only one could eat at a time. Adult male rats are about 30% larger than females, are stronger, and are more aggressive. So you might expect the males to dominate these scarce resources. Yet the females got an equal share, and more. In four separate colonies, females monopolized the feeder almost 60% of the time.[1] Milk chocolates, considered a special treat, were eaten by females 70% of the time.[2] Such findings are startling, indicating not just parity between males and females but the clear subordination of male survival to female survival.

Investigators at the Calcutta Zoological Garden severely limited food rations for a mixed-sex troop of rhesus monkeys. Given that male monkeys are larger than females and are more often violent, what would you expect? The male monkeys are surely strong enough to shove the females aside and hoard all the food themselves. Yet it was the younger male monkeys who lost weight, so much that two adolescents almost starved and had to be removed and rehabilitated.[3] When vital interests clash, females and ranking males feed while lesser males starve.

Animals act as nature programs them to act, and nature programs these social animals to act in a chivalrous manner. Yet if these were human societies, a similar bent to sacrifice males so that females can survive would be considered highly noble. Clearly, in understanding competition for food among these hungry animals, chivalry stands out over size, brute strength, or general aggressiveness.

So too in human communities that face starvation. Perhaps the most famous is the Donner party, which set out across the Sierra Nevada mountain range in October 1846, headed for California. Stranded by unexpected snows, these pioneers passed the winter together, exhausting food supplies and eventually resorting to cannibalism. Of the 82 pioneers trapped in the snows, 35 died of starvation and hypothermia.[4] All but one of the first 14 to die were vigorous adult men, who had exhausted themselves wrestling the wagons across the mountains.[5] In all, 52% of the males died, compared to 29% of the females.

Pioneer girl Laura Ingalls writes of a terrible winter with provisions running out and the family near starvation.[6] "Pa," facing demanding physical labor and losing weight, insisted that the others share the food. This should not surprise anyone. Any community has a few scoundrels, but the normal man does not hoard the provisions while his wife and children go without. Where survival is concerned, a chivalry toward females seems to be embedded in humans as well as in other animals.

We are rightly concerned that men might use their physical strength to ensure their own survival, while women perish.[7] Yet such an arrogant arrangement would hardly survive. We might imagine an odd tribe somewhere, ten thousand years ago, in which the men freely hoard as much food as they can eat and the women and children subsist on table scraps. Inevitably, when food runs low, the men eat everything and the women and children starve, leaving our imaginary tribe with no progeny and no next generation. Among our actual ancestors, men surely supported their women and children, which is why they are ancestors and not the last of a now extinct race.

Male competition and female choice

Most of us have seen pictures of bucks locking horns in struggles for dominance, and so we naturally assume that the males dominate everyone. Yet we must look at the pattern of male aggression. Males aggress selectively, not against females but against other males, to maintain their territory and for sexual access to the females. Bucks fight against other bucks but not against the doe, who graze contentedly and then mate with the winners. So while we observe that males are usually the dominant social animals, we must recognize that the other males are being dominated, more so than the females.

A roughly similar pattern is seen in human society, although it is not as tight as we might wish. Men are more aggressive, but the most severe male aggression is against other men. In fatal confrontations, three quarters of those killed by men are other men.[8]

Some have objected to parallels between animals and humans, concerned that male domination among lower animals could be used to justify continued male domination in our own society. Observations that females are benefited take us away from those earlier concerns and on to challenging new concerns.

Why are males programmed to concede to females where vital interests are concerned? Male acquiescence might be considered generous, and surely is, but its origins lie in the brutalities of genetic selection. Look at an evolutionary explanation:

Males who assault females and hoard vital provisions would seriously imperil the next generation of offspring, thereby harming their own genetic interests. In competitive situations, the stronger males prevail at the expense of weaker males, but the dominant males seldom benefit by allowing their females to starve. Indeed, dominant males benefit instead by supporting females, preventing peripheral males from taking their food or harming them. Obviously, the females must survive to carry the dominant male genes into the next generation, while the peripheral males are marginal or irrelevant.

Most groups of mammals have more than one eligible male, giving females a say in which males mate and which are rejected. Female choice of mates is apparent among many species of birds and mammals, including most primates.[9] Among chimpanzees, for example, lower-ranking males are observed to give way to females during feeding, to win their cooperation later for clandestine matings.[10] A young male monkey who pushes a female aside and steals her food is not going to be her first choice for a mate. The young male who offers her his share of the edibles promotes his own genetic heritage.

So regardless of whether dominant males control mating or whether females choose, male genes benefit from supporting females. A dominant male benefits by favoring reproducing females over subordinate males, while an average male benefits by supporting females who might choose him as a mate.

Recall that among chimpanzees, male chimps ordinarily have higher rank than females, but nonetheless give way in squabbles over food. Male genes gain from higher status, more so than female genes, so males fight harder for public respect.[11] But when vital interests are concerned, these same males defer to the females, whom they must rely upon to propagate their genes.

In our own species, as we shall see, men generally support women and try to protect them against rogue men who would harm them. A typical man also tries to provide for his wife and family.

Chimpanzee knights in shining armor

Chivalrous alliances are seen among chimpanzees as well. In one incident, a threatened female chimp calls upon a male companion for assistance. Using high-pitched barks, she points toward her assailant with her whole hand (rather than just a finger), at the same time kissing her companion and patting him. As her pleas become more insistent, he charges out to battle her antagonist while she stands by and watches approvingly.[12] Thus is rescued another damsel in distress, and her champion becomes the hero of the hour. Call him Champ Chimpski.

Chivalry is not merely a personal choice but also a social imperative, and Champ here acts to uphold an unspoken standard of justice. Like a real man, although a shave short in stature and light on brainpower, he enforces one of our highest and noblest moral callings. He stands by fair maiden, and uses his power to punish the dastardly scumbag who has so callously offended her.

A chimp such as Champ who supports the damsel may gain opportunities to mate with her later, while one who refuses his support will also be remembered and treated accordingly. And so too among humans. Men who uphold women against offending men gain their respect, and perhaps their favors, while men who ignore women lose out. So nature programs men to support women in distress and to stand strongly against the beastly bastards who cross them.

Chivalry among social animals does suggest that chivalry originates in the lower and more primal areas of the brain, and surges forth without an excess of rational consideration. Thus, we can act in a highly chivalrous manner with little more forethought than we might expect from that good fellow Champ Chimpski.

Men Risk their Lives for Women

We now admire plucky women who work in macho fields, as undercover police officers or jet fighter pilots, but we are all more comfortable when men take the actual risks so that women remain safer. National figures show that 94% of on the job fatalities are men, and only 6% women.[13] Even correcting for more men working than women, that is about a ten to one ratio of male fatalities to female fatalities. The ten most dangerous jobs today have been listed as logger, small aircraft pilot, fisherman, steel worker, garbage collector, farmer and rancher, roofer, power line worker, trucker, and taxi driver.[14] Communications tower worker tops some lists. If we include the macabre, we should add in suicide bomber as well. Men hold all or almost all positions in each of these highly perilous occupations.

Men are much more inclined to take risks than women, in our own culture and around the globe.[15] And we all expect men to face the sorts of job hazards that we would be unwilling to push upon women. Chivalry is also seen in our unquestioned acceptance of these practices. Would any of us want to argue that women should take more of the perilous jobs so that men might be safer? We have not heard any women argue for equal risks, and it would be hard to respect any man who is foolish enough to do so.

We see human nature not just in those positions we argue, but also in those positions which are so solidly accepted that it makes no sense to argue either for them or against them. We feel so strongly that men should sacrifice themselves to protect women that it would be unthinkable to try to turn the arrangement around.

Why men sacrifice for women

Why do we feel so strongly? Life for our ancestors was often perilous, and men frequently risked their lives to hunt game,[16] battle nature, and battle other men. Women favor men who are willing to sacrifice for them, now as always, and men also favor comrades who share the sacrifice.

Imagine Enga and Org in a primitive hovel eighty thousand years ago, enjoying a roasted rabbit when a poisonous snake slithers in out of the cold and invites itself to share the meal. Suppose Enga screams and Org steps forward, as we would expect, and he battles the viper and saves his wife and the children. Enga admires her protector, and the two continue as mates.

Now step into fantasyland for a moment and imagine that Org were a coward, and that instead of stepping forward he runs, leaving Enga and the children to fend for themselves. Perhaps Enga whacks the snake, or perhaps a handsome woodsman from the adjoining hovel hears her scream and comes to her rescue. Either way, Enga refuses to giggle again with Org and awaits for her chance to giggle with the handsome woodsman instead. And when word of his cowardice gets around, no other woman will have Org, not for love nor money. Men benefit from protecting women, and those who fail to do so also fail to mate and do not pass along their unchivalrous genes. Men must be willing to protect their women if they are to continue their genetic heritage.

In contrast, women would gain zero genetic advantage by risking their lives for men, and women are little inclined to do so. The courageous woman who saves her man from the snake has just saved a loser, and the woman who is injured trying to save her man imperils her children and her own genetic heritage. Women sacrifice themselves to protect their children, which is in their genetic interest. So the simple process of genetic selection, working over millions of years, accounts for why men risk their lives for women and not the other way around.[17]

Shipwrecked

In 1912 when the Titanic set sail for America, men held all the positions of formal power. The steamship owners and managers were men, as were the Captain and the principal officers and those who manned the lifeboats. Of the women on board, most had no right to vote and only after several years and a monstrous world war would women gain that fundamental right throughout America (1920) and in the United Kingdom (1918 & 1928).

As the unsinkable liner slipped under the waters in the wee hours of April 15th, how much did all of that matter? With lifeboats in short supply, the men chivalrously allowed women to board first, many voluntarily and some because the men in charge required it of them. In all, 74% of the women passengers boarded the boats and survived, while only 20% of the men boarded and the remainder perished in the dark, freezing waters of the north Atlantic.[18]

So we see again a substantial separation between men and women. As with human cultures generally, even when men monopolize all the positions of formal power, we can see that women still retain significant advantages.

War sacrifices men

Military battle surely involves more injury and death than any other human activity, and is conducted almost exclusively by men. In peacetime, women might serve admirably in military command and operations. Where we expect serious battlefield casualties, we place the women in the safer areas of service. Women want the choice to serve, but not even the strongest feminists argue that women should be conscripted and *forced* to fight and die, as men often are.

Egalitarianism among Israelis and the callous indifference of Joseph Stalin have sent women into combat, but neither nation regularly sacrifices their women today.[19] In modern armies, in any nation around the world, women are given safer assignments mainly in support of the fighting men. The number of women soldiers among the American dead in Iraq have been mercifully limited to just over 2%, while women comprise about 15% of the American military.[20] So the fighting men take about ten times the risks as do the women. As far as we know, no human community regularly sacrifices its women to its enemies, so long as men are available who can be sacrificed instead.

Strength is still an obvious asset in modern warfare, although most women could learn to fire an assault rifle or drive a truck through a barrage of exploding shells. The essential quality is the willingness to submit to military authority, out of honor and loyalty to comrades. A soldier must be willing to follow battlefield orders at the risk of being shot up, blown apart, incinerated, gassed, drowned, speared, stabbed, stoned, or bludgeoned to death. Soldiers are men because men can be trained to sacrifice themselves in ways we would ordinarily not expect of women.

Murderous misconduct

At the extreme fringe of what we might euphemistically call marital misconduct, women murder their husbands or have them murdered almost as often as men murder their wives (almost a thousand each way, per year).[21] Yet we feel violence by men against women is substantially more immoral than is violence by women against men. A national Department of Justice survey found that Americans rate a woman stabbing her husband to death as 40% less severe than a husband stabbing his wife to death.[22] So if we rate the man stabbing his wife as a ten, meaning truly heinous, then the woman stabbing her husband is just a six, meaning still serious but perhaps more understandable.

Such moral standards leave us dumbfounded. A man harming a woman is surely more reprehensible than a woman harming a man. But why? Our feelings go one way, our sense of equal consideration goes the opposite way, and our reasoning struggles to sort it out.

Our moral sentiments here arrive by the same familiar paths as other chivalrous concerns. Our ancestors would select a man by whether he could be counted upon to support a woman, just as we do today, but select a woman on her youth and appearance, just as we do today. A man who whacks his mate has shown himself to be a worthless scumbag and is hardly a man at all, whereas an attractive woman who happens to whack a man is still very much a woman, although a tad risky. Men are ordinarily willing to take risks for women, and a woman who has just lost her husband may be quite available. Over the generations, our genes spread when we rid our villages of malicious men, and also when we make some allowances for misguided women who might still bear children.

We can provide various rationales to make our judgments appear sensible and fair-minded, but our moral standards here clearly reflect our ongoing genetic interests. If we are dumfounded by such findings, it is because they come to us through our primal heritage and are indifferent to our higher intellectual reasoning.

Clans Set Standards

It seems reasonable to be concerned about men exploiting women, while it would be odd indeed to crusade against women using men. However commonsensical, we might still ask the obvious question: What makes us feel this way?

Immediate family and close relatives matter among humans, as opposed to orangutans or hard-working border collies. In all cultures, up until our highly mobile modern era, individuals tended to hang together with immediate family and close relatives and to look out for each other.

Close relatives share many of the same genes, and so relatives have a genetic interest in the mating activities of all of the youngsters. Just as a boy who marries a girl and stays to raise their children thereby benefits her family genes, a boy who impregnates a girl but bails out on her has exploited the girl and cheated her family out of the necessary assistance. A pregnant girl may fall back on her family, but she thereby stretches their resources and reduces their competitive advantage. So parents, siblings, cousins, and the whole clan have a genetic interest in a daughter being treated properly. The family wants to see that any boy who is with a daughter is good to her and can be counted upon to support her.

A boy who impregnates a girl can be forced to marry her and support her, and the shotgun wedding at the business end of a spear would have been one consequence of fooling around, hundreds of thousands of years before the shotgun was ever invented. The cost of taking advantage of a girl can be truly severe. Early records provide frequent instances in which fathers or brothers took up arms to pursue and slay a false suitor who betrayed a daughter or sister.[23]

Families are not so concerned about a son who has a casual romantic adventure. He is just sowing some wild oats. Male genes can benefit from casual liaisons as well as from committed ones. Nor is the family always so concerned about whether the girl is treating him like a prince or is screaming at him. It is better that a son be with *some* girl, even if she is mean to him, than with no girl at all. Any girl can transport the family genes into the next generation.

So our inclination to protect our women from bad men provides a major genetic advantage, whereas zealously protecting our men from bad women would be genetic folly. By selecting those sensitivities that promote our genes, nature programs us to be outraged by men exploiting women but to remain somewhat oblivious to women exploiting men.

When a fellow marries a girl and takes on the responsibility for caring for the children, his family expects her to be faithful and is morally outraged if she is sneaking around with another man. We tend to overlook it if a daughter-in-law is crabby, but our tolerance quickly vanishes if she is unfaithful. An unfaithful woman cuckolds not just her husband but his family as well, as the whole clan can be wasting its resources in bringing up a genetically unrelated child. Where men and their relatives can control mating, penalties for female infidelity can be severe.

The double standard

The traditional double standard that allows casual sex for males but not for females applies only to those within our clan. For outsiders, it reverses itself. That is, the double standard allows a woman from elsewhere to have casual sex with a grown son or a brother, but stands adamantly against a man from elsewhere who wants casual sex with a daughter or a sister.

Suppose a 19-year-old young man courts your 16-year-old daughter, has sex with her, and then jilts her and goes upon his merry way. We are all civilized folks, but many of us would be bitter and we would feel like smashing the fellow. Now suppose a 19-year-old-girl courts your 16-year-old son, has sex with him, and then jilts him and goes upon her merry way. Many of us would object, but it would be an unusual parent who would want to smash the woman. We protect our women from sexually exploitive men, which makes sense, more than protecting our men from sexually exploitive women, which would seem odd indeed.

Chivalrous sympathies can provide additional genetic benefits. A man who stands up for a mistreated woman against her man will gain favor with her and with her female friends, any of whom might transport his chivalrous genes into the next generation. A man who stands up for a mistreated man against his wife will lose favor among her female friends, reducing his chances of mating and imperiling his genetic future. The risks are huge, and men are programmed to avoid them as much as possible. Women who stand together also set the standards of conduct for their communities, thereby protecting themselves.

Innate moral sympathies

In our era of easy birth control, many can accept it when a woman friend sleeps with her lover or even lives with him, so long as she is content with the arrangement. Yet the moment she is upset and complains, she triggers our chivalrous programming. We are outraged, and we want to help her to get rid of the bum.

The implication is that our natural human concern for the welfare of females is not a reversible social convention that could have just as easily been otherwise. It is not as if the founding forefathers wrote into the Constitution that men should support and protect women and our society has been this way ever since. Our concern for females goes much deeper. It resides in our innate natures, and surges forward when females are mistreated or distressed.

Chivalrous sympathies guide gender socialization as well. We uphold men who support women and are outraged by men who harm women.

We expect men to be dominant, but we feel strongly that men *ought* to support and protect women rather than oppose them. In that important sense, the man who defers to his wife rather than argues against her is doing what he ought to do.

In *The Moral Animal*, political scientist Robert Wright argues that evolution shapes not only our actions but our moral sympathies and moral conduct as well.[24] In *Origins of Virtue,* Matt Ridley argues convincingly that our various standards of moral propriety and fair play are not simply imposed upon us from afar but are reflections of human nature itself.[25] In *Moral Minds,*[26] Marc Hauser shows how nature programs us with an onboard sense of right and wrong. Among those who look carefully at human nature, a growing consensus says that moral sensitivity is woven into the very fabric of human nature.

In *Manhood in the Making,* anthropologist David Gilmore looks closely at numerous primitive and industrial societies and concludes that in all cultures, men are highly protective of their female mates.[27] We see here that chivalry is not just a Western anomaly at all but appears consistently across cultures in any era and anywhere around the world.

The point here is surely not that all men are chivalrous, or that the average man is chivalrous twenty-four hours a day. Men can be alcoholics, bullies, deadweights, swindlers, rapists, and almost anything else under the stars, and societies can be openly unfair in controlling women in various ways. The point here is that overall, in various important situations, across cultures everywhere, communities tend to be to be more protective of women and more punitive toward men than the other way around.

Chivalry provides men and women each with our own unique challenges.

⚲   As a man, you should realize that anger counts more strongly against you than it would against a woman. Your anger is hardly a manly response to her anger, and it will cost you severely. You do not have to consider it fair to realize that chivalry is the prevailing standard. Be a good sport about it. See your station as an opportunity to replace anger with wisdom, and to become more conscientious and more compassionate. Use it to become a better man.

Being gentle toward women and slow to anger is an essential feature of manhood, and is a worthy achievement. While women are more argumentative and show more anger, recall the finding that men remain stressed and bitter after quarrels longer than women. Working to resolve that bitterness is surely a worthy objective, lest it seep out as sarcasm or emotional withdrawal.

♀ While garnering more sympathy can provide an immediate win, it carries with it a lingering cost. The same chivalrous standards that support you and uphold your grievances also allow you to be reckless without knowing the harm you do. Your challenge is to avoid indulging in your complaints, and to try to be more balanced and more understanding of your opposites.

A Modern Maladaptation

Chivalry seems to have functioned over hundreds of thousands of years to hold families together, obligating men to support their wives and children and punishing men who fail to do so. So long as a woman requires support from a man, then whatever we do to force that man to support her is apt to be helpful. Yet surprisingly, as society prospers, the same standards that have glued marriages together can now act in reverse, to tear marriages apart. When a woman is relatively inde-pendent, then automatically supporting a woman against a man creates an oddly maladaptive inequity.

Parenting rights

While men and women do not gain the same advantages from relation-ships, we would expect that relationships are best when we benefit jointly and about evenly. In one major arena, parental rights to the children, the courts traditionally have granted women custody of the children and financial support, promoting a highly chivalrous standard. As of the 1990's, mothers have been the primary custodians in about 65% of divorces and men the primary custodians in 10%, along with various forms of shared custody arrangements.[28] Regardless of who we feel should raise the children, even if we feel that mother knows best, we should agree that having the right to raise your children must count as an advantage over not having that right. So we have an opportunity for a research question. If we could provide men and women with more equal parenting, removing some of this one chivalrous inequity, would it improve things?

Given that we cannot wave a magic wand and arbitrarily alter our legal arrangements, how do we answer the question? Good fortune seems to have smiled on our research project, as some states have moved toward more equitable custody for fathers, while other states have not. So the state legislatures and judges have waved the magic wand for us, and we have only to tally the results.

In those 19 states with available figures, the more frequent use of joint physical custody arrangements in 1990 was followed by decreasing divorce rates over the next five years, compared to states which mandated sole custody typically to the mother.[29] The strength of the findings is substantial. The more frequent use of joint physical custody arrangements accounts for fully 22% of the changes in divorce rates.[30]

Joint and equal parenting arrangements also reduce feuding between divorcing parents. When one parent will be strongly preferred over the other, then divorcing moms and dads fight viciously over who will be preferred and by how much. In joint custody arrangements, where we can expect to be treated about equally, men and women are more inclined to agree and less inclined to drag it out and squander limited funds on continuing litigation.[31]

Bitterness between parents is always hard on children, and continuing bitterness during and after a separation is especially harmful, particularly when parents fight about the children.[32] Anything which makes a separation more amicable will surely benefit the children.

Joint arrangements also allow children to maintain full access to both parents, and children do considerably better in joint custody arrangements.[33] While the courts often assign custody to the mother, children do better when fathers participate equally in their activities.[34]

A general policy of equal parenting rights for both parents improves marital stability, reduces animosities between parents who do separate, benefits the children and makes a separation easier on them, and allows custody lawyers a much needed respite from their demanding legal work loads. It is not without its problems, as parents often try to nickel and dime each other on who has a child which hours on which days. Yet when fathers want to remain involved, we might figure that a strong preference for joint custody would be a no-brainer.

Yet we have two competing standards here. Obviously, we want what is fair for everyone and we want to do what is best for the children. But chivalry is programmed strongly into the human animal, and we feel that it is highly moral to uphold women and to punish the men who wrong them. So we tend to side with women in their hour of greatest need. Our inner Champ Chimpski charges in to support the fair damsel in distress and to punish the worthless lowlife who has wronged her. Legislators craft the guidelines, judges side with women against men, and as voters we go along with the whole arrangement.

While chivalrous inclinations have conscripted men to the support of women and families over the ages, bonding families together, we see here how those same inclinations can also weaken marriages and undermine fatherhood. In our modern times, the same chivalrous wiring that once held us together can now escort us apart.

Here as elsewhere, our reasoning suggests one path and our feelings carry us the other way. We should like to think that reasoning and good sense can eventually prevail, and sometimes it does. More courts are now adopting joint custody, but the legal system changes slowly. Mothers remain the primary residential custodians in the vast majority of divorces.[35] Yet you do not have to wait for your local courts to gain the benefits of an equitable parenting plan.

Agree together that in case you might separate, you will follow a joint and approximately equal plan for parenting your children and supporting them financially. If you really mean it, write it down and sign it. If you do not want to have to think about a divorce, look at the advantage: Your equal parenting agreement will increase your chances of staying married and lower the chances that you will have to actually experience later what you want to avoid thinking about now.

Not all inequalities are created equal

Note here that various chivalrous policies can have opposite consequences. Men sacrificing to protect women is so wired into our genetic heritage that sacrificing women instead would be unthinkably abhorrent. When the sacrifices men make are acknowledged and honored, then the additional respect might actually promote stronger relationships. Our one suggestion, which may be too unrealistic, is that the popular media mention that men are the ones who make these ultimate sacrifices, so that women might be more inclined to respect men and so that we might all benefit from more appreciative relationships.

Courts supporting women and siding against men is also chivalrous, but it has the opposite consequence, undermining families and turning us against each other. Chivalry can benefit our communities when it involves men supporting women and children, but chivalry can also poison families when it promotes inequitable solutions that turn women against men and remove men from families.

We introduce here the somewhat novel principle, that not all inequalities are created equal. It is not as though each and every unequal feature is a festering blight on our land which must be ferreted out and abolished. Some inequities seem benign or at least neutral, while others undermine relationships and tear at the very fabric of the culture. Our aim is not just to identify various contrasts between men and women, but to try to be sensible about which of them matter and why.

The importance of our various customs rests not on whether they are strictly equal, which many are not, but on whether they serve the interests of our communities and promote better lives for all of us. We need to look not on whether each man and each woman has equal rights in each and every aspect of life, which is an impossible goal but sparkles for us just out of reach like the pot of gold at the end of a rainbow. Instead, by judiciously granting rights and assigning responsibilities, we should seek to benefit men and women jointly and equally, to strengthen our families and our communities. Our social philosophy is thus broadly communitarian,[36] placing our mutual interests ahead of those individuals who look out only for themselves.

೧೩   ೩೦

4.

The Master Illusionist

A lie gets halfway around the world
before the truth has a chance to get its pants on.
— Sir Winston Churchill

Given the widespread influence chivalry has on so many aspects of our lives, an alien from another world might assume that we humans recognize that human society is generally supportive of women. Even if the space alien looks just like the rest of us, he is so far off that we would quickly realize that he is from another world. Our alien friend would have to delve much further into the matter in order to understand why we ourselves fail to understand.

Most of us believe that society is not chivalrous at all, and believe instead that human society is sexist and that we oppress women. A Gallup poll finds that 73% of Americans believe that society is biased in favor of men and against women.[1]

The contention that men do not support women is a product of our modern times. A half century ago, it was generally accepted that most men toiled and sacrificed to support their wives and children. Men who provided well for their women were considered respectable, in spite of their flaws. Criticism of men stayed closer to home and out of the broader public eye, and was aimed more narrowly against those men who were fools or lazy or who drank or chased skirts or otherwise failed to provide for their women and children.

The Tilt against Men

One can hardly escape the sense that American society is becoming increasingly critical toward men.

In a 1970 survey, women were most likely to call men "basically kind, gentle, and thoughtful." In a similar survey in 1990, women more often described men as only valuing their own opinions, trying to keep women down, preoccupied with getting women into bed, and not paying attention to household affairs.[2]

Recent research suggests that overall, our contemporary opinions of women are generally more favorable than our opinions of men.[3] Is that a surprise? Women are more often seen as socially sensitive, friendly, and concerned about others, whereas men are seen as dominant, controlling, and independent. Our current views mirror somewhat the English and American attitudes in the early Industrial Revolution, where women were thought to create homes of "peace and concord, love and devotion," while men strived in their work realms of "selfishness and immorality."[4]

The introduction referred to a recent Gallup poll in Great Britain that finds that 33% of women "often or very often" feel resentful of men, compared to just 14% of men who often feel resentful of women.[5] So fully a third of women carry with them an ongoing resentment toward their opposites, as compared to just under half that number of men.

Traditionally, perhaps the most important contribution a man can make to his family is to provide for their financial and material needs. Men provided something in hunter–gatherer societies, and considerably more so since the beginning of agriculture and the various civilizations which followed. Men were the "breadwinners," and "brought home the bacon," while women ran households and raised the children. While the Industrial Revolution opened jobs for women away from home, men remained the primary providers.

Women in the American workplace now earn about 75% as much

per hour as the working men. We have traditionally respected men for their higher earnings, but no longer. Today, women who earn less are considered oppressed, and the men who earn more are therefore turned into the oppressors. How quickly the fundamental contributions of men tumble, from honorable breadwinner to sexist oppressor.

So too with fatherhood. Traditionally, while mothers often set the household standard, fathers were respected as contributing parents and expected to maintain order and back up mom in squawks with the children. That too has vanished. In one early survey, only a slim 11% of mothers reported that they value their husband's input on how to handle the children.[6]

In *Men in Groups*,[7] originally published in 1969, anthropologist Lionel Tiger provides an optimistic portrait of the bonding between men that makes task groups run smoothly. In *The Decline of Males*,[8] published thirty years later in 1999, he provides a morose portrait of men today as dazed, confused, and lacking confidence in themselves.

The recent tilt against men rearranges our minds and then surely rearranges our relationships. Why should a woman want to try to fashion a lasting relation with a man, when she now sees him as an oppressor rather than a provider and she figures he has so little to contribute to a family? And why should a man take on the responsibility, as the woman has so little respect for him and he cannot see any way he will ever earn her respect? The tilt against men surely contributes its share to the current swing toward fatherless families.

Why the tilt?

What is changing? The traditional pattern was for men to work in agriculture and industry while women maintained the home and raised the children. Women now hold influential public positions in universities, in the various media, and in our political and legal machinery. Influential women are everywhere in public life and are carrying their grievances against men into the broader public consciousness.

Women have always been more outspoken in personal quarrels, as far back as the research can take us, while men tend to concede, placate, or withdraw. Sprinkle our naturally chivalrous sympathies into the mix, and our public conversation becomes almost uniformly supportive of women and increasingly harsh toward men. Women express one outrage after another, while men keep their mouths shut and try to stay out of trouble.

As women gain more rights and more opportunities, we might expect that the new equality would soften their anger. Yet what we observe is just the opposite. As women gain more formal power, their anger spills out more powerfully into the public consciousness.

In *Who Stole Feminism,*[9] philosopher Christina Hoff Sommers sees pioneer feminists as wanting equal treatment and career opportunities, while the more militant feminists who followed see only their own grievances and ignore equal consideration. Militant feminism casts itself as social innovation, but it is merely using the traditional female anger advantage against the more civil men and women who stand in its way.

> A man defending husbands vs. wives or men vs. women
>   has got about as much chance as a traffic policeman
>   trying to stop a mad dog by blowing two whistles.
>
> — Ring Lardner

The social proprieties that incline us to support and honor women for their special qualities are now stronger than ever. While men have been traditionally honored for their strengths and virtues, being openly supportive of men has now become somewhat improper and unsuitable for mixed company, as it might imply that men are better than women in at least a few select ways. Being openly critical of women is socially improper now, as it always has been, while being publicly critical of men is not merely tolerated, as it has been over the ages, but has gained a beachhead and is pressing forward. The tilt involves touting half of the controversies, supporting women and criticizing men, and suppressing the other half. As we look at only one side of the story, our biases morph into an absurdly lopsided sense of reality.

Chivalrous Misunderstandings

The modern tilt against men strongly biases our impressions of men and women.

Do women work harder?

Take the widespread belief that women usually do more of the work overall while men watch more TV. In *The Second Shift*, Arlie Hochschild and Anne Machung sympathize and offer advice to overworking women.[10] We often hear about women who have jobs outside the home and then do a second shift of housework and childcare while their husbands watch football. So we too naturally assumed women are busier. Is it so?

An early University of Maryland study tracked over 5,000 Americans and found that we have about equal free time: men have 41 hours of free time a week and women have 40 hours.[11] A University of Michigan study, looking at jobs, commuting, childcare, housework and yard work, found that the average husband works 61 hours per week while wives average 56 hours.[12] Another Michigan group found that around the world, men averaged 16 hours of housework while women averaged 24 hours. Men also average 37 hours of paid work outside the home, while women average 24. If anyone is keeping score, that means that men total 53 combined hours of work, while women total 51 hours.[13]

With these findings in mind, we can think of any number of men we know who work all the time while their wives have more manageable schedules. So it balances out. The number of women who overwork more than their husbands about equals the number of men who over-work more than their wives. We acquire a biased impression because women who hold jobs and do the housework complain about how unfair it is, and publicize their grievances,[14] while overworked men are not supposed to complain. It may be little consolation for those women who do more than their fair share, but the findings do show a balance between the sexes.

Our biased impressions contribute to one rift after another between men and women. Why should a young woman go through all the hassle of establishing a relationship and getting married, when she believes that she is going to have to do more than her fair share of the work anyway? And why should a young man sign up to marry, if he has figured out how much work is required of him and how little he will be appreciated for it? If women really did do more than their share of the work, than that would be unfair and should be changed. But men and women do about equal work, and the whole problem is a cruel misunderstanding. Here as elsewhere, chivalrous illusions make relationships even more difficult than they would otherwise be. Each misunderstanding is only a single pebble on the mattress, but a whole handful of misunderstandings makes for a poor place to sleep.

Most of us might assume that those who complain the most are being treated most unfairly, which may or may not be so. It is an acrobatic feat indeed to see beyond our lopsided complaints and chivalrous proprieties, to find some semblance of equal concern for men as well as for women. Might we suggest that you try?

Why men earn more

Return to the finding that women earn only three-quarters as much per hour as men earn, which we hear repeated again and again with the implication that society is biased against women. In *Why Men Earn More*,[15] popular author Warren Farrell shows that the salary gap is fully accounted by the nature of the jobs men and women take on. Men take on tougher, riskier, more specialized, and less pleasant jobs and work more hours at them, while women take more comfortable jobs with better security and spend more time with their families. Men more than women choose jobs with 70 hour workweeks and endless travel away from home. Of mothers with graduate or professional degrees, fully 54% choose not to work full time, trading in the wear and tear of the fast track for the personal satisfactions of the family track. Farrell shows that women who take on the same risks and the same hardships as men earn fully as much as men (or slightly more). *Why Men Earn More* has been a featured title of the American Management Association.

On average, men scientists earn over twice as many patents as do women.[16] In another era, men might gain some respect for their substantial contributions to our technological progress and material prosperity, but no more. We now interpret men being more productive as a solid sign that the system discriminates against women. Yet universities and corporate labs surely want all of their scientists to succeed, regardless of race, creed, color, gender, or religious persuasion.

Women who are convinced that the workplace is biased against them have every reason to confront the alleged perpetrators and try to extract fair compensation. So here as elsewhere, our chivalrous sympathies contribute to another misunderstanding that angers women, promotes contentious lawsuits, and furthers the tilt against men.

Physical confrontations

The same chivalrous standards apply strongly to our more ordinary physical confrontations. While we think of domestic violence as men assaulting women, scores of surveys invariably find that men and women report similar frequencies of assaulting their opposites and of being themselves assaulted. While figures vary, a midrange estimate is that 12% of men and women in a relationship physically confront their partners. [17]

And it all begins so early. A 2006 CDC Injury and Violence Prevention report finds that among high school students, 8.9% of boys and 8.8% of girls report being slapped, hit, or otherwise assaulted in a relationship.[18]

Most of these confrontations are more ordinary acts such as grabbing, pushing, or slapping, while some are more serious. The most serious offenses, which involve beating up on someone, occur in less than 1% of relationships.[19] A quarter percent of women reported needing medical care at some time for a partner injury,[20] and far fewer men, suggesting that severe injury is relatively infrequent.[21]

So overall, as many as 50 couples engage in some form of physical confrontation for every serious injury.[22] Why so much physical confrontation compared to so few serious injuries? Most of these men are not intending to injure, and most women are not strong enough to injure even if they meant to do so. Those who physically confront each other ordinarily do so to underscore an argument and to get their way, but not to seriously harm the other. While it is easy to sensationalize physical confrontations, we might note that most incidents involve commonplace features such as grabbing, shoving, or slapping, and a much smaller number injure or are meant to injure and are therefore properly considered violence.

While frequencies may be similar, our chivalrous natures judge similar acts according to widely separate standards. A man hitting a woman is a moral abomination and should never be permitted, while a woman hitting a man seems more a lapse of proper manners or perhaps a justifiable emotional outburst. We are outraged by men assaulting women, but hardly give it a second thought when it goes the other way around.

A man who throws a drink of whiskey at a woman has assaulted her, and men have been prosecuted for such. In contrast, a woman who throws a drink at a man is merely expressing her outrage. What sort of wuss would call the police and try to prosecute a woman over a splash of whiskey?

Battered men file police complaints only a twelfth as often as do battered women,[23] and so seldom come to our attention. Here again, our accusations follow our genetic interests. What sort of fool would hand his wife over to the men in authority and probably lose her, just because she takes a swing or two? A woman, on the other hand, must count on a man for her safety, and she benefits from punishing the reckless egotist who goes too far over the line.

Off Balance

Relationships are confusing enough anyway, and chivalrous standards simply multiply the confusion. Most of us consider it right and good and proper to support women and to avoid offending, and we hold men accountable who offend women. So, while unflattering critiques of men can be justified and are somewhat commonplace, similarly unflattering critiques of women are considered sexist and improper and are tightly censured.

Our chivalrous natures thus magnify some concerns, minimize others, and distort the relationship between men and women. We must recognize the lens, to avoid being taken in by its familiar images. Only then can we look around it to see gender concerns clearly. Our clumsy emotional programming has not the vaguest chance of figuring it out on its own.

One of our editors told us that we provided more advice to women than to men, creating an obvious bias. We had thought that we handed out the advice about evenly. So we tallied up our advice sections for women ♀ and those for men ♂. The book you are reading has 23 advisory comments for women, 28 for men, and 19 for both. It just appears that we are asking more of women. We are so used to asking men to change for women that suggestions that women change for men seem oddly improper.

How do we strike a compromise between social propriety and balanced inquiry? Be we wise or foolish, witty or boorish, none of us has ever argued that we can understand any complex matter by seeing only one side of it.

Improper realities

We have competing standards. On one hand, ideally, we should be truthful and say what is important. On the other hand, we should be sensitive and proper, and avoid the comment that offends, however true it might be. We are expected to be truthful, meaning that we should not lie to those who might find out and object. But we are well advised to avoid offending, even though it means telling courteous little lies and pretending they are true.

The book in your hands may be forthright to a fault, and the authors have never been accused of being flatterers. We believe that the willingness to understand ourselves and laugh at our folly indicates strength of character and promotes growth. The truly inquisitive will appreciate the suspended world of uncensored observations here, where our intuitive understandings can be explored and confirmed. Many of us will see here what we already suspect, and will benefit from having our intuitions confirmed. You have the opportunity to step away from the masquerades, clear the cobwebs from your minds, and gain your bearings. We expect we might all benefit from it, each in our own time.

Candor is indeed a mixed blessing. Candor may be uncomfortable at the moment, but then beneficial in the long run, whereas flattery is enchanting in the moment but hardly a basis for wise choices. Candor invites censure, which is why so many of us avoid it, although communities ordinarily benefit from candor and pay dearly for their self-serving illusions. A relationship is itself a two-person community, and a proper sprinkling of candor has a real chance to benefit those who can open their hearts and minds.

Some of what we look at here may seem improper or totally blinky. So be careful with what you learn here about men and women, and use it wisely. In the best of all worlds, truth and balance would be offered wisely and accepted graciously with no offense taken, and we would all prosper without being overly false. In our actual world, we must weigh truthfulness and balance against the prevailing proprieties and the cherished illusions.

Our illusions can be confusing indeed, at first glance. And then, as we look around, adjust to our surroundings, and get comfortable with these worldly realities, we can abandon our dowdy pessimism and allow intrigue and fascination to carry our spirits upward. What spellbinders these illusions prove to be!

♂ ♀   The more we know, the more careful we must be to walk safely amid those who do not know. Open your own mind, learn, become wiser, and grow old. But be careful about how much of it you reveal, and when and where and with whom. Always consider when you can talk freely, and when you will be misunderstood and censured.

Smoke and mirrors

The hand of the illusionist is standard and not at all complicated. While the illusionist captures our attention with the empty hat, he positions the doves behind a mirror or inside his sleeve so that they will magically appear to fly out and wow us at the just right moment. What he shows us is merely to hold our attention, so that we do not see what is going on behind the scenes. Similarly, the master illusionist that is chivalry invites us to look at one side of our moral universe while brushing away or hiding from us the other side, creating the illusion that moral concerns between men and women go only one way.

So far as we claim society is sexist and treats women unfairly, we thereby commit ourselves to advocating better treatment for women, which is indeed quite chivalrous of us. Were we to argue that society is chivalrous, and that men do indeed support women, we thereby suggest more respect for men, which would be oddly unchivalrous.

Saying that men oppress women is now a rallying slogan, staking a strong claim that men *owe* women more consideration, more support, more rights, more advantages, better protection, and more money. Include the proper implications, and recognize that the conviction that men oppress women is itself an argument for more chivalry.

Those three-quarters of Americans who believe society is unfair to women reveal that their own sympathies are for women. While not realizing that chivalry even exists, we nonetheless reveal its hold on our minds. The few who judge society to be more evenly balanced show how relatively unpopular it has become to remain neutral.

We are now expected to compliment women on their multiple talents and many achievements, while it is considered sexist and terribly improper to notice limitations or moral failings. And it is now also improper to honor men for any special strengths and virtues, as it can offend women, and it is also commonplace to condemn men for the many ways men mistreat women.

We are all familiar with magicians who make coins and cards appear, and make glamorous ladies and even tigers vanish. But how many of us have seen a magician make himself vanish and then remain invisible while he continues to produce his artful illusions?

Paradoxically, oddly, bizarrely, our chivalrous nature itself is behind the impression that we are no longer chivalrous. The same chivalry that allows us to publicly criticize men but not women produces an atmosphere critical of men, and thereby paints the impression that our culture is supremely unchivalrous and callously unfair toward women. Chivalry thus has the quirky quality of masking its own presence and of producing the appearance of its opposite. What a grand master of the masquerade!

Civilization

It is said that men have contributed everything that is wrong with civilization, which is close to the truth. Men pioneered about ninety percent of everything that is good and bad or simply mediocre in every civilization known, while women ran the homes and brought up the children. Men are indeed the architects of our cruel wars, our grinding inequalities, and those interminable committee meetings whose sole purpose is to schedule the next meeting.

We cannot imagine men without women, as we would have no next generation of children. But we can take a look at other species, to fashion a guess or two on what life would be for women without men.

Among orangutans, for instance, a family consists of a mother and her children. The mother provides whatever the youngsters require, while the male shows up only to mate but otherwise goes his own way and lives a solitary life in the forest. Here the males do not benefit the females, but neither do they control or oppress in any way. It is a wonderfully matriarchal arrangement in which the females live completely free of male interference and do not have to rely on their male counterparts to invent the wheel or to install indoor plumbing.

Who Gets to Be Right?

"You cannot be right and still be happily married," according to a wise old saying. It has the ring of truth among pastors, psychologists and marriage therapists alike, and with almost everyone who has ever been in a fruitless marital squawk. Here's the logic: As long as you feel you are right, and you argue your position relentlessly, on and on, the chances are slim indeed that you will remain happily married.

And yet, something is missing. Is the problem the fact that you are right, or that you argue on and on and refuse to listen?

We need to amend the saying: "You cannot be right and argue it relentlessly and remain happily married."

So many arguments are about who is "ever so right" and who must be therefore "oh so wrong." Many of us feel that we must be right, as though our survival depends upon it, and that our spouse must agree with us to confirm it. And we argue on and on refusing to yield on any of the particulars. We want to be not merely right, but completely and totally right.

Suppose I feel misunderstood by my spouse. Must I necessarily prove that I am right? So far as I myself am convinced that I'm right, then can I stop arguing, let it go, and not convince anyone else of the supreme justness of my cause? Once I do that, the argument is over.

Do you require someone to agree with you in order to be right? Do you require validation? If so, you must continue an argument, even a futile one, or you will automatically feel wrong. But if you do not require someone to agree, then the world opens up before you, and you have choices.

You take a step back and buy some time. You might tell your spouse that you hear what he or she is saying and will think about it awhile, and get back to him or her. Or you can say that you are not sure about your own opinion, that you want to weigh out the questions and consider where you do stand, and that you will review the question and then continue the discussion. The latter is merely a longer and more proper version. Either way, you gain the time to figure things out in your own mind before you must tangle with your opponent.

We do listen more, now that we are older and supposedly wiser, and surprise! Since we are no longer fighting foolishly for the right to be right, we are freer to slow down, step away, and do some actual thinking. And often enough one or the other of us sees that we are *not* right, or that we both have good points, and we concede more graciously.

Note we might have two quite separate concerns in any argument: We want to know what is so and who is right, of course. But we should also look at what is worth saying, if anything, that will improve matters and will help us understand and reconcile. We can indeed be right, but realizing we have no way to convince an opponent, we keep our own council and wait for a better opportunity. Conversely, unfortunately, we could be wrong, run over an opponent, and so win, but still be just as wrong as if we had lost.

In the world of masquerades, the one who wins the argument gets to be right. Step behind the masquerades, and it is another world entirely.

Realize that being right has nothing to do with being able to argue longer and louder than your partner. So, figure out what is so and where you stand; and then figure out what you can say that might be understood.

The first is a matter of truths; the second involves practicalities. Understand what is so important, and then be practical. We offer some advice along the way, to point us toward friendlier relationships.

If, as you read this, you are trying to figure out whether men are right or women are right, you have missed the whole point. If you can pretend for a short span that you do not have to be right and others need not be wrong, you will have a much easier time of it.

Begin Where You Are

If half of crafting a loving relationship is convincing our opposites to do as we wish, the other half is learning to accept and appreciate each other the way we are. We hope that seeing how men and women evolved helps us better appreciate the quirky ways we act toward one another. All the better if it can provide a smile or two or even a grimace along the way.

> … grant me the serenity
> to accept the things I cannot change,
> the courage to change the things I can,
> and the wisdom to know the difference.
>
> — Reinhold Niebuhr, the Serenity Prayer

We present here the most intimate masquerades, which we invite you to enjoy in all their magnificent splendor. If a journey of a thousand miles begins with the first step, get your bearings on where you are now and then venture forth with that first step. Look forward to the walk itself, and not just to your final destination.

 Be content with small steps, which is all anyone ever gets anyway. You cannot reconcile opposing wills with one miraculous insight or one especially profitable night of argument. Rekindle the fire carefully, without burning the house down.

ॐ ॐ

Part III.
Tangled Together

The emotional bonding and social obligations of relationships are comforting to many but confining to others. Nature did not introduce pair bonding out of the goodness of her heart for our simple pleasures. The human pair bond is a viable program to raise surviving youngsters, as it is in only a few other species of mammals but in most species of birds. The wondrous joy of a new romance, the strains of making it work, and the pain of infidelities and abandonment are all components of a broader scheme.

Obviously, each of us wants our fair share of the advantages or maybe slightly more, which seems only fair. So who contributes how much, and is that enough? Who is getting the better deal, and who is being shortchanged? We look next at how we communicate and at the hidden nuances of gender patterns.

CR   ℘

5.

Twisted Communication

"I know you believe you understand what you think I said,
but I doubt you realize that what you imagine is not what I meant."

— Unknown

You might almost suspect that we all have the same problem. You hear it again and again: "We don't communicate!" The most prominent complaint among modern marriages should not be such a surprise. Modern couples seek warmth and intimacy above all else, and we naturally figure that good communication is the golden path to intimacy. Good communication is not everything, of course, but it is important.

What is the point?

Consider first not *how* we communicate, but *why*. Do we say things simply because we feel them, to express ourselves, and then expect to be understood? Or do we say things carefully, in order to clarify, calculating what to say and how to say it, so that we will be understood? Do we say something *because* we feel it, or do we speak *in order to* craft a better relationship? Our feelings are sometimes our friends, but not always.

♂ ♀ So far as you consider your feelings vitally important, you might speak your mind because you feel that way, to express your feelings. So far as you cherish your partner and your relationship and feel called to resolve concerns, you might be more careful, speaking in order to understand and to be understood. Your answer here is a window into your communication problems. Look carefully at your priorities. Is it better to say what we feel, or to consider where we want to go and figure out how to get there?

In emotional confrontations the intensity of feelings, the fast pace, the ego and pride, the overblown accusations, and the failure to listen all combine to create a mirage of illusions and misunderstandings. Indeed, angry arguments are themselves dustbowl masquerades, in which the legitimate concerns are often concealed behind blind posturing and wild improvisation.

It is worthwhile to focus on communication, to clarify the intentions, correct misunderstandings, provide more positive alternatives, and ensure that both parties participate.

Say now what you mean now!

So many arguments are over what was said in an earlier argument. While you assume you remember, or pretend you do, we suggest otherwise. After listening to hundreds of accounts of arguments, we conclude that it is unusual for either partner to have more than a whisper of insight into the garbled miscommunications that get us hot and then keep us frying. We assume we know what we said, but injury and anger are players themselves and not impartial witnesses. And we argue that we know what our opposites said, which we ignored even then as we sought to prepare our own points and argue them.

"He said, she said" is not a court record. She says, "You said," he says, "I never said," she says, "Now you say you never said?" he says, "Say whatever you want," she says, "I say it because it is true," he says, "Whatever."

Are you following it so far? Is it a plagiarism issue or a copyright violation? The argument seems to be over whose words are being quoted or misquoted and used without permission for slanderous purposes. Each of us wants to rehash what was said, feels the other is fantabulating, and does not realize it is all a pretense and that neither of us really remembers what was said or done. How do we resolve a quarrel over something that we cannot even agree ever happened?

♂ ♀   ADVICE: If you find yourself tangled up in accusations about past statements, stop. Forgive the faulty memories and remove yourselves to the present. Think about what the issues are now, and figure out where you stand now. To whatever you said earlier, plead no contest. Say what you mean now.

Try: "I'm not sure what I said earlier. I'm saying now that I am willing to ..."

Or: "If I said that, I'm sorry. That's not what I mean. What I want to say is ..."

Why play out a re-creation of an earlier presentation that had such unsatisfactory results? Your concerns are with you right now. Figure out where you stand and what you want to say now. Each new conversation should be a chance to write a better script.

Listening

How well do most of us listen? Within what is broadly termed "trouble communicating," most of the problems are not from failure to express feelings but from the failure to listen and understand.

Cross-complaining

The most common marital miscommunication is at least 98 percent talk and less than 2 percent listening. In *cross-complaining*, also called *counter-complaining*, each partner ignores the other and voices his or her own complaints. One expresses a grievance, the other responds by expressing a grievance, and so on. Here are some typical "he says, she says" snippets:

> HE: You're going through the money I earn faster than the federal mint can print it.
> SHE: You think you're really funny.

> SHE: You never get home when you say you will. How can I plan supper?
> HE: You always find something to complain about. If it's not one thing, it's something else.

> HE: You never act like you want sex. You never initiate anything.
> SHE: Nothing I do is ever enough for you. I quit trying.

> SHE: You never talk to me.
> HE: Remember what the marriage therapist said? You should never say "never."

These conversations seem normal enough to the intensely involved participants. But just reading them can bend your mind. Do you find them confusing? In each case, the response is close enough to the initial comment to almost pass, but it completely disregards the expressed concern. Yet we become so comfortable with cross-complaining that we hardly notice the complete madness of it.

Listen first

Why do we pay so little attention to what someone else says? Blame it on natural egotism, which wants to put oneself first. Most of us want to speak first and be heard. Then, perhaps, we would be willing to listen as well.

There is an advantage in reversing the natural order.

 Listen first, and say something to indicate that you have heard what your partner says. Then, in all fairness, you can ask to be heard in return.[1]

In many cases, it works. By patiently listening and showing you under-stand, you often take the angry edge off of an argument. And we do need to understand the opposing position to figure out whether to agree, bargain, compromise or hang tough. Most arguments fail not for the lack of argument but for the lack of an audience.

Acknowledging what your partner says slows arguments down to a maddening crawl, which is a second benefit. The more we slow down, the more time we have on our hands to consider what we want to say and how to say it well.

Hotheads will absolutely hate the slow pace, and will not continue it for long. Too bad.

 Work to be sure your audience stays on your side, and you will be astonished how much power your arguments will carry.

If resolving conflict is the key to compatibility, then listening is one key to conflict resolution. Really listening means more than just watching the words go by, waiting for the chance to jump in and counter with your own opinion. It means listening attentively and accepting what is said, even critical comments, without being offended or stressed by them.

> … grant that I may not so much seek
> To be consoled as to console,
> To be understood as to understand,
> To be loved as to love.
>
> — Prayer of Saint Francis of Assisi

All that might be too idealistic for our modern tastes. Yet if even a few of us really bought into the message then we would not have a fraction of the strife we face every day.

When you never thought about listening

Many have never tried listening because they never thought it was important:

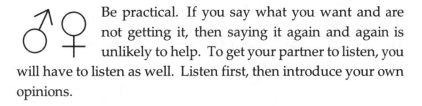 If that is all it is, you are in luck. Yours is the easiest problem to fix. Realize how important it is. Reread the comments above on cross-complaining. Talk to your partner about whether you add complaints upon complaints, and how often you do it.

Think of one or two times you spoke before you listened. Ask yourself what you missed by not listening. Need help? Ask your partner what you missed by not listening.

Arrange with your partner for each of you to check how well you are listening. Converse about something — anything. As you do, rate yourselves not on how much you say but on how well you are listening. Who is listening better? Who rates most improved? Do you know why your partner rates you as he or she does? Are you listening?

When you want your own way

Some do not listen because they have more important things on their minds — like expressing their own feelings and pushing for what they want:

Be practical. If you say what you want and are not getting it, then saying it again and again is unlikely to help. To get your partner to listen, you will have to listen as well. Listen first, then introduce your own opinions.

Pushing for your own way is also boring. Since you focus only on your own feelings and your own arguments, you never see the full picture. Perhaps you think you are tired of the relationship and are lonely because your mate does not understand you. But by listening to yourself repeat yourself, you are boring yourself witless. Listen to your partner and see what you have been missing. Even if you do not get your way, you will surely find the conversation more interesting.

Lower Stress Quarrels

Researcher Howard Markman concludes that the quality of a relationship depends on how well you are able to handle negative feelings, particularly your partner's expression of negative feelings toward you, toward the relationship, and about life in general.[2] Obviously, feelings of being insulted, injured and severely stressed impair your ability to handle conflict. Can you stay calm in conflict? It is vital to staying focused and resolving grievances.

Some marrieds argue forcefully for what they want and still remain relatively unstressed in conflicts. These pairs usually fight fairly, stating what they want without accusation. Just as important, they also understand how much the other can manage. Each wants the argument to work out well all around, and each tries to ensure that it will. Just as the tension becomes unmanageable, one may crack a joke, concede a point or two, offer a compliment, or acknowledge that he or she goofed. Partners are aware enough to see when they are doing harm and concerned enough to try to make amends.

Suppose he has been pushing too hard, and she gets her feelings hurt and starts to cry. "You aren't listening again," she says.

He sees he has hurt her feelings and that she is about to stop talking to him. So he smiles, then concedes. "I do have a problem listening. Could you repeat what you just said?" And this time, he listens.

How many of us are sensitive enough to see when we are taking an argument one step too far?

"By the rules"

Howard Markman and collaborators suggest rules for talking and listening and ask couples to handle sensitive communication "by the rules."[3] In the "speaker–listener" technique, only one partner speaks at a time while the other listens. The speaker presents his concerns, and the listener then paraphrases what she hears. It helps the listener to better focus on the message, show she is listening, and correct any misunderstandings. The two trade off having the floor, alternately expressing their own concerns and trying to understand the other. The more volatile the subject, the more important it is to go by the rules.

Some of the rationale for using rules is based on gender differences. Research indicates that when conflict occurs in games, girls are more likely to break off the game while boys are more likely to clarify the rules or make up new rules to keep the game going.[4] Among girls, the relationship is more important than the game, whereas for boys, who relate primarily through activities, the game *is* the relationship. The rules that allow boys to manage conflict in sports and games are obviously missing in most marriages, setting the stage for men to withdraw when conflict occurs. Women can manage the unrestricted emotional exchanges that men find unmanageable. Introducing rules into heated conversations levels the playing field. Rules allow men to participate instead of being overwhelmed, so that women can have a partner who talks and listens instead of withdrawing.[5] Admittedly, most couples do not talk this way, even those in satisfying relationships.[6] Yet Markman's conflict management training is somewhat successful in stabilizing marriages, suggesting that we can get along better when we hold onto a few simple rules.[7]

Men and women have different ways of listening or, more importantly, different ways of failing to listen. Look here at some of the obstacles that stand in the way of hearing one another. Several of these occur more in one sex than the other, although any of us can stumble over them.

Taking it too personally

Those in vital relationships are usually able to accept criticism without taking it too personally. When we are overly sensitive and unwilling to accept criticism, we limit what our partners can say without causing harm. Oversensitivity to criticism suffocates communication.

We talked with a fellow who wanted to find out how his marriage had gone so wrong and how to patch it up. His wife judged him to be emotionally unavailable and was considering leaving him. He told me that he had felt close to her when they were first together, and that she had been attracted to his charm and his joy of life. How did things change so much? He identified a critical incident, which occurred just after they were engaged. She told him he was not a good kisser, and she proceeded to instruct him on how she wanted him to kiss her. He took her comments as broad condemnation, viewing her as controlling and something more—perhaps "vicious" would not be too strong a word. He remembers mistrusting her after that, and he withdrew emotionally from her. He went through with the marriage, but this incident, and a few similar ones, severed what had been a warm bond of affection. And she grew increasingly unhappy with his aloofness.

We had occasion to talk to the wife. Yes, she was bossy. But she was also intelligent, organized, attractive and sexually responsive—which was what attracted him to her in the first place. Were he to have been comfortable with her occasional criticisms, and maybe even have agreed to kiss her as instructed just to please her, he could have been more happily married. Overreaction to occasional criticism is lethal. Easy acceptance of contrary opinion is necessary for understanding and compromise.

The man had been genuinely injured when his fiancée told him he was not a good kisser, and he failed to get over it. How many women would be that hurt by such an ordinary comment and so unable to shake it off?

Are you oversensitive when your mate is upset or critical? How does your mate rate you? He or she may be in a good position to know. Or ask some of your friends or other family.

Try the following one item test: Rate whether you agree, disagree, or are not sure:

o   When you speak in anger, you say what you really mean.

If you believe a few words spoken in anger reveal a broader inner malice, you are taking anger far too seriously. Words spoken in anger need not be any more or less important than words spoken out of appreciation or concern. An angry comment may be just blowing off steam.

See a moment of anger as a mere blip on the video screen. You will be more comfortable with your mate and with everyone else as well.

Shield out hostility

The implication is that to better manage conflict, we do well to become more comfortable with it. Unfortunately, the advice itself does not usually help. Stress reactions are mainly autonomic and not under conscious control. We suggest stress reduction training to help stay calmer in conflict situations. In the *Personal Shielding*[8] training, you stretch and relax, construct a shield in your mind, and then practice using your shield to deflect hostile comments. Those who practice shielding stay calmer later on, in hostile situations. A solid 80 percent of those who read the booklet and listen to the training cassette are clearly calmer in conflict over the next several weeks. Lower stress allows you to listen better, think more clearly, answer cordially instead of angrily, and resolve conflict instead of being swept along by it.

Insistence and Misunderstanding

The man who does not talk much about his feelings poses a challenge to the woman who wants to understand him. Yet the obstacles are not insurmountable. Most men respond to a good listener and will provide enough personal information to splice together a general sense of what is going on. The challenge is to be a good listener.

With so many women wanting more communication, you might think that women would be primed to listen and understand whatever men manage to say. Alas, such is not the case. You would be surprised at how often we hear a woman complain that her husband never talks, and then observe that she does not hear the first word he says when he tries to tell her something. Any woman who can out-argue her husband can easily get too involved with her own winning argument to take much interest in his losing argument. The same holds for the man who can out-argue his wife, although women are typically more comfortable arguing.

"I don't understand why..."

We sometimes complain about not understanding something, as though we want an explanation, when what we really want is a change. Both genders do this, although women seem to do it more often. Look at some examples:

> "I don't understand why you can't remember a card for Valentine's Day."

> "I don't understand why you can't talk to me about your feelings."

> "I don't understand why you have to buy so many shoes."

The ambiguity is in the word "understand," which has two meanings. "Understand" means "to comprehend with your intellect," as when a child says, "I don't understand why the sun comes up in the East." He wants an explanation about how the earth spins counterclockwise so he can pass the science test. "Understand" also means "to accept, condone, or tolerate," as when the same youngster says, "I don't understand why I have to go to bed at ten o'clock." The last thing he wants is a sufficient explanation, and no explanation will suffice. He wants to stay up. And he is saying that unless you can give an acceptable explanation—and no explanation will be acceptable—then he should get to stay up. It is a way to pester you into conceding to what he wants.

Saying, "I don't understand why you can't remember a Valentine's Day card," sounds like a question, but it is really a complaint. You are irritated that your mate did not remember. You are grilling him for not remembering, and you have a right to make him squirm. No man is going to score points trying to explain why he cannot remember a card, and he knows it.

Masquerades, anyone? The "Why" and "I don't understand why" comments are typically complaints masquerading as questions. The beauty is that they seem to be questions. Your opponents try to answer them as questions, tangling themselves up in an impossible proposition.

Eventually, an opponent becomes wary and refuses to participate. So we score with the impossible question, but then we lose in the long run. Confused by our tangled accusation and annoyed about being grilled, we produce resistance and opposition.

♀ (& MEN TOO): It is better to be a bit more forward about what you want. Or, if you cannot bring yourself to make another request, at least tell him you are annoyed with him and tell him why.

You just don't understand!

A similar analysis applies to "You just don't understand." An exasperated woman who says, "You just don't understand!" might seem to mean that her fellow is not comprehending the problem, but it is more than that. She is also saying that the issue is important to her and that she means business. She is saying that he is not taking her concerns seriously enough and, until he does, she is fed up with his insensitivity and is not interested in talking to him further. "You just don't understand" puts him on notice that the issue is no longer negotiable and that it is up to him to concede or else face a continuing standoff. "You just don't understand" is a woman's expression, meaning only that women use it considerably more often than men.

A man may "understand" her position but not agree with it or not want to comply with what is expected. The admonition pits one will directly against the other, and the sturdier combatant has the advantage. "You just don't understand" is a woman's expression because men tend to fold in these sorts of battles and try to stay out of them.

Overblown Accusations

We have all heard that we should never say "always" and "never," but we all do so anyway. As is so often the case, the source of the problem lies in an illusion concealed even to ourselves.

One who feels neglected and wants more conversation says, "You never want to talk to me!" One who feels left out and wants more consideration says, "You always think of yourself first!" The man who wants sex more often says "You are never interested in sex." Why do we so mindlessly create such untruthful exaggerations?

Anger usually expresses itself as an accusation against whoever we feel mistreated us. Anger says that we are justified, and that our opposite is wrong and ought to concede. Of course, anger wants to hurl the strongest accusation possible. Anger tends to focus narrowly on what someone has done wrong and to present it in the worst possible light, exaggerating the case and ignoring the opposing arguments entirely.

Angry confrontations are intensely involving, as we uphold our own justifications as if our very survival depended upon it. Unfortunately, we are taken in by our own arguments. It is said that a press secretary tells wild tales of convenience to gullible reporters, sleeps soundly, then comes to believe his own tales when he reads them the next day in the newspapers. Similarly, an angry person presents overblown justifications to strengthen his own case, but convinces himself as he argues them so convincingly. Attitude research confirms that as we prepare a position and argue it aloud, we become more convinced of its merits.[9]

A woman yells tearfully at her husband that he does not love her anymore. She is not merely expressing her feelings. She is scripting and participating in an intensely involving experience. As she accuses, she experiences the misfortune she is portraying. She feels the emptiness and the terrible injustice of it all. While her accusation is aimed at her husband, it afflicts her as well, leaving her as injured by it as he is. The more she repeats it and the more convincingly, the more she wounds herself with her message.

Why so much anger? Women often feel that their husbands do not hear them until they get really mad.

Overblown accusations create a vicious cycle that maintains itself. We feel unfairly treated, we nurse our grievances, we make overblown accusations, we believe our own propaganda, we feel more mistreated than ever, we become angrier, and so on. By strengthening its sense of justification, angry accusation fans its own flames. Here too, in some odd way, the posturing passes for reality. We create the masquerade of righteousness, and then convince ourselves that it is true.

The Gottman research finds that women tend to escalate arguments friendship. Find a way to repair the breach, and go back to being friends.

CR ℘

while men more often try to defuse them, meaning that women are more apt to use overblown accusations than are men. Yet many men use overblown accusations as well, and the same insights and advice apply to all of us who overstate our grievances.

Why use an overblown argument, when a balanced argument might do just as well and cause fewer hurt feeling? We use "always" or "never" in an argument because these words seem to make an accusation stronger, more forceful, more final. One who *always* does something is obviously the culprit and has no leeway to squirm out of it by claiming that it was just a few times, or inadvertent, or not very important.

Yet the "always" or "never" words usually make an argument more brittle, not stronger. Since these accusations are usually not true or not completely true, your mate can easily dismiss them as simply false, overlooking the important issues contained within. Because they seem unfair, overblown accusations offend, generating counteraccusation instead of understanding and resistance instead of cooperation.

And therein lies the illusion. We believe our overblown accusations are stronger and we hurl them with mighty force, while a more balanced commentary would be more apt to create a solution. Overblown accusations are clumsy and therefore weaker than we imagine.

It does not help as much as we would wish to be more clever or more forceful. We need to be fairer, and then clarify our positions and persist with what we feel is actually fair. One way to soften anger is to gain a clearer and more balanced sense of the grievances that produce it:

♂♀ Try to state your grievances carefully and fairly, without exaggeration. In doing so, you do not weaken your position but make it stronger and more credible. You might also try to balance your own concerns with those of your mate, which makes it more likely that you will be heard.

Instead of saying, "You never talk to me," say, "I realize that you do talk to me, and I appreciate it, but I want more. Could we spend some more time together and just talk?" Your more civilized request is likely to get a more civilized response.

When you are careful with the truth, you also clarify your own thinking. You rebalance the mental scales that you use to weigh your relationship. You come to see your grievances for what they are—important, yes, but not always the catastrophes you were blowing them up to be.

Those who make the most outrageous accusations may have trouble making the simplest and most reasonable requests. They may feel they should not complain about small matters, so they reach too far and make it all too important. Lacking confidence in amateur boxing, they take up nuclear weapons.

Are you able to state your position, and argue for it, simply because you want it your way or feel strongly about something? Or must you turn it into an intolerable injustice before you can say anything? Better to stay with the simpler issues and argue them with confidence.

Can you argue on your own, or must you call forth your anger to argue for you? Better to argue it yourself. Anger is an overzealous ally which stirs up more trouble than it is worth.

Overblown accusation can slide easily into paranoid accusation. Feeling mistreated, we blame someone for *wanting* to hurt us and doing so on purpose. Sound familiar? He works late without calling and shows up late for dinner. She is worried and upset. She says, "Why do you want to hurt me like this?" He may be working late to get ahead, and maybe because he dreads going home as well. But men do not work late for the explicit purpose of upsetting their wives. By personalizing the offense, she makes her grievance more forceful.

Understanding an overblown accusation

We usually object to an exaggerated accusation, and argue against it:

SHE: You are always late!
HE: I am not *always* late. You are being ridiculous!

She does not recognize that by exaggerating, she has translated an

important personal concern into a literally false commentary. He does not recognize she has said anything that is true or worth saying. She can do better, of course, but he can too!

When you answer an accusation, even an overblown one, be sure to address the actual feelings. When your partner gripes that you are always late, try to overlook the "always" and focus instead on the legitimate concern.

"Well surely not always," you might say, "but you are saying that I am frequently late, which is so. And that it bothers you. Let me think about it for a moment and figure out why I am having trouble being on time."

People tend to repeat themselves until they feel understood. By hearing the message, you lower the pressure your partner feels to continue forcing it upon you. You may move past the accusation, and go on to negotiate and perhaps resolve the concern.

Repairing and Remaining Friends

Romanticism involves seeing the best in your partner and cherishing your idealized image. Compassion is seeing someone as he or she really is and loving him in spite of the flaws, or perhaps even more so because of them. Over time, it is the amount of compassion rather than the romantic flavoring that makes or breaks a marriage. We tend to focus on the wonderful qualities when we fall in love, but each of us has our shadow sides as well.

However we argue, whether we listen to each other calmly or fly off into the stratosphere, it is important that we find some way to recover from an argument and remain friends.

It is essential to reach out, with a touch of warmth or understanding or humor, or an apology, to say that we really are friends and that we matter to each other more than the argument matters. And when one of us reaches out, it is essential then that the other accepts the gesture and reaches back.[10] An argument is a breach in a

6.

Unevenly Yoked

We might easily surmise that men, who are more interested in casual sex and who generally want more personal space, are simply not as involved in relationships as are women. The prevailing opinion is that men are less willing to commit and are the ones who most often walk out on relationships. Yet what we observe is just the opposite.

Jilters and jiltees.

Men seem to bond more strongly than women, take it harder when relationships fail, and take longer to recover. Women make the final choice to end relationships considerably more often than do men. What is going on?

Among serious couples, whether dating, engaged, or married, in any decade sampled, women initiate a separation or divorce more often and typically about twice as often as do men.[1] Court records show that wives file divorce petitions almost twice as often as do husbands.[2] In 1986 women filed 60% of divorces, men filed 30%, and the remaining 10% were filed jointly. The same trend is seen amid the much lower divorce rate of an earlier era. Court records from 1931 show that 70% of divorces were granted to women, compared to 30% granted to men.[3] A 1950s look at engaged couples found that the women folded the engagements almost twice as often as the men, usually out of interest in dating another man.

The observation is not unique to Western cultures such as ours but is seen around the globe. In the former communist Soviet Union, with its obese social welfare system, women filed seven out of ten divorces, citing alcoholism as the primary reason.[4] Similarly in Japan, known for its traditionalism and social stability, women also initiate seven out of ten divorces.[5]

The woman may not be the first to want out. A man who wants out may stay, out of obligation, waiting for a woman to hand him his walking papers. Women who want out feel freer to leave, other considerations permitting. Yet it is not simply that men are usually the ones to want out and wait for their opposites to agree. Among dating couples, a woman with strong feelings for her partner is typically more able to leave an unpromising relationship. A fellow with strong feelings finds it harder to let go, even when his girlfriend is no longer interested in him.[6] Some boys continue to wait for a girl who is going out with other boys, too much the fool in love to break the bonds and try to go on with a life without her.

Couples separate for various reasons, of course, but one scenario is somewhat typical. The wife feels dissatisfied, pushes for more communication, is angry, and wonders if she wants to stay married. The husband resents her complaining, withdraws emotionally, and considers leaving her, but feels obligated and cannot abandon her. The standoff continues. When she has had enough and no longer loves him, she weighs her options carefully, makes her decision, and asks him to leave.

How about extramarital relationships? By our own tallies over several decades, the men who make the choice to leave almost always have another woman, whereas the women who make the choice may or may not have another man. Several of our colleagues have offered similar observations. Even here, we see again how strongly men depend upon women. Men depend on another woman to leave a marriage, whereas women can act more independently and leave on their own.

Men are supposed to support women, most of us agree, and women have a right to be supported. So when a marriage fails, a woman feels cheated of the support she has a right to expect. A man is troubled by failing in his responsibility and leaving his wife so hurt and upset. So women usually feel mistreated and angry more than ashamed, while men tend to feel ashamed and inadequate more than angry. Anger helps you leave a relationship, of course, while obligation burdens you and holds you back. Those who fit this pattern far outnumber the exceptions.

Counter to ordinary expectations, men are more deeply hurt by separations than women. Men tend to cling longer to dying relationships and fantasize longer about their former partners after it is over.[7] On average, men take about twice as long to recover from failed relationships as women do.[8] In short, men get their hearts broken more often than women and take longer to heal.

Married men are also healthier and happier than single men, and they work harder and achieve more. Somewhere around 90% of highly successful men are married, whereas closer to 70% of highly successful women are married.[9] Men find meaning and purpose in supporting a wife and family and are often lost without it.

By one survey, men who divorce get remarried two years later, on average, while women who divorce get remarried about six years later.[10] These quicker remarriages are often attributed to men having more opportunities. Yet a recent poll of divorced singles finds that 66% of men but only 51% of women say they want to get married again.[11] The higher percentage of men who want marriage suggests that there should be surely enough men for the interested women. Men are more eager to remarry, while women are usually willing to take their time and consider their options more carefully.

A man whose wife dies is ten times more likely to commit suicide after the loss than is a woman whose husband dies.[12] Regardless of how independent he appears or how independent he imagines himself to be, the average married man is profoundly dependent upon his relationship with his wife.

The difference shows up as well in our expressions of frustration. Exasperated women say, "Men! Who needs them?" Exasperated men say, "Women! You can't live with them, you can't live without them!

It shows up in our public truisms. "A woman needs a man like a fish needs a bicycle," according to a catchy phrase popularized by Gloria Steinem.[13] In contrast, "A man without a woman is only half a man," according to an old Jewish saying.

Note also that the individual who can least manage the loss is normally under more pressure to capitulate. In a study of engaged couples, men more than women reported frequently giving in to a fiancé for fear of losing his or her affection.[14] The trend seems to continue solidly into marriages. Husbands are more apt to concede in arguments, fearing that their wives will be upset and angry or unbearably cold toward them.

Interviews with a hundred stably married couples turned up several instances where women used rational ultimatums, often successfully, that forced a husband to choose between changing his conduct or losing his wife and family.[15] Yet none of the men had used similar ultimatums with a wife. Anyone can threaten in the heat of an argument. But few men are brassy enough to give a wife a serious ultimatum and then leave or throw her out if she refuses to comply.

Equality and stability

The observation that women are the ones who more often fold relationships also helps explain why equal treatment for men in separations helps stabilize marriages. If men were the ones who typically bail out on marriages, then social arrangements which support women and punish men would act to hold men to their commitments and would stabilize marriages. Since women are more typically the ones to bail, preferable treatment for women who leave simply makes it easier for women to leave. Remember that somewhat more equitable joint custody arrangements accounted for fully 22% of the reductions in divorce rates over a five year span. We might surmise that preferable judgments for women contributed a fair share to the steep climb in divorce rates in the 60's and 70's.

What is it that bonds men more strongly than women?

Relationships Obligate Men

Even a few brief interviews with men lead us behind the masquerades. A normal man experiences some sense of obligation to a woman with whom he is intimately involved. Whether he graciously accepts it, grudgingly resigns himself to it, frets about it, ducks it but feels ashamed, or rises above it, the concern is there. A man wanting casual sex typically worries that the woman will take it too seriously and expect a commitment, making him feel obligated to her.

The average woman may be concerned as well about her obligation to the opposite sex but not as intensely as the average man. Instead, she worries about whether her fellow really loves her and whether he takes her seriously. Most women are hardly aware of the tremendous power that obligation holds over men or of its many implications for a relationship. Men are aware of it all the time.

After a relationship fails, a man can be more worried about how his ex–wife is doing than he is about himself, even when the ex– is managing well and he is coming unglued. The sense of obligation that holds men in relationships can severely punish those who leave.

Sex itself obligates men more than women. So far as we see sex as a benefit that women provide for men, then the woman who provides the favor is not obligated to continue to provide it whereas the man who gains the favor is reasonably expected to provide her some special consideration in return. So the woman who provides the favor and bails out is merely making a choice, although we might consider her a player, where the man who receives the favor ought to commit something.

Feelings of obligation should not be confused with love. A man may be bored with a woman, or even find her obnoxious, and still feel obligated to her. The unfortunate consequences can slide into unintended comedy.

In a student sensitivity training group, a freshman told one of the girls in the group that he was attracted to her but that he did not want her to be too involved or expect too much from him. She told him not to worry, she hardly knew him. To her, his concern seemed unflattering and inappropriate, which indeed it was. He was trying to duck out of any responsibility for her feelings for him even before she had any feelings. Sadly, for the young man, his sense of obligation was a ball and chain of his own making.

We hope those feelings settled out for him before he tried marriage. If a guy feels so obligated before he even knows a girl, imagine how he would fare as her husband.

Origins of obligation

The obligation a man feels toward his wife is ordinarily as strong as that he feels toward his children, and often stronger. In contrast, the strongest sense of obligation a woman feels is usually toward her off-spring. Why do men feel more obligated toward women than the other way around?

Perhaps surprisingly, obligation provides an evolutionary advantage for a man. The man who stays and supports his wife and children provides a substantial advantage to his own progeny, while the man who abandons the wife and children imperils his own genetic legacy. The obligation that compels him to stay can tip the balance when he finds the relationship unpleasant and would wish to be free of it.

Obligation is also a social expectation, with the accompanying pressures to comply and the punishments for those who shun their responsibilities. Sex produces babies, especially before our modern era, and the babies and the women who bear them must be supported. A man was judged harshly who seduced a woman and then moved on, and the consequences have been severe indeed. Families of a wronged women are known to take up arms and attempt to slay the false suitor.[16]

Marriage in some form began about 1.7 million years ago, anthro-pologists surmise, and has been customary among our various ancestors since then.[17] If an average generation spans just over 20 years, men would have had about 75 thousand generations to adjust to the advantages of bonding. Agriculture began about ten thousand years ago, and in agricultural civilizations relatively lasting marriages became the norm and have continued until modern times.

Could a man not have more offspring by staying single and sliding from one woman to the next? How much does marriage handicap his mating opportunities? In our modern permissive culture, surveys show that married men have more sex than single men. We doubt it was ever otherwise, and the strict and punitive cultures that prohibited extra-marital sex would render the average bachelor celibate most evenings with few romantic liaisons and few progeny or none at all. Sanctioned sex in a committed relationship would ordinarily translate into more children than would holding out for the occasional unsanctioned tryst.

So over the millennium, bonding strongly to a woman has meant more sex, more offspring, more support for his offspring, and the respect of the community and the advantages it confers as opposed to the many perils of the exploit and run tactics. Is it such a surprise that an onboard sense of obligation toward a woman produces surviving offspring who carry that inclination into the succeeding generations? And in what is called a mixed reproductive strategy, a man who stays married may still chance an occasional unsanctioned tryst.

In contrast, a woman who must rely upon a man for support and protection has enough practical reasons to stay with him, so that a strong sense of personal obligation toward him would be irrelevant. And if she is with a poor man or slacker who cannot or will not support her, and she can find more advantageous arrangements, then she and her future children may indeed benefit by leaving the poorer mate and accepting the better offer. A stronger sense of obligation to a mate would be a smaller genetic advantage, and nature has programmed it more softly into women than men.

It has been suggested that unattached women do better than un-attached men because women have more intimate friendships and talk more openly about their feelings. Maybe so. But nature could have programmed men to be more independent—or even totally independent, like panthers, hunting alone and completely content with no companionship at all. Male dependence on women provides an obvious genetic advantage, holding men in relationships to support their wives and children.

Imagine a primitive community in which men feel free to leave when they get offended and are self-sufficient enough to live out on their own. If their wives complain too much, these men go out to hunt, eat what they bag instead of bringing it back to camp, tell jokes over the campfire, never worry about their wives, and never come back. Their women are free to mate with other men who will provide for them, but may suffer hardships. Either way, the genes for that sort of rugged masculine independence are not long for this planet.

Why we fool ourselves

The common opinion that women are more emotionally dependent than men is merely another facet of the masquerade. Here is how we fool ourselves:

Women talk about it when relationships fail, and companions see how upset they are. Males usually suffer in silence, and their grievances go unnoticed. A jilted woman triggers our chivalrous sympathies and we naturally want to support her. When a man gets jilted we figure he did not have the right stuff. A man jilting a woman is a moral transgression, whereas a woman jilting a man who does not meet her standards is more of a personal choice. And we remember what concerns us most. In folklore and cinema, the tale of a sweet woman in love with a ruggedly independent man appears more often and is certainly more appealing than a tale of a sweet man in love with a ruggedly independent woman.

It may seem paradoxical that males appear aloof but bond more strongly, while females seem more intensely involved but feel freer to leave. Perhaps the explanation is in the paradox itself. The sense of being overly committed already makes men wary of further commitment, while women are freer to pursue intimacy because they worry less about being trapped by it.

A woman ordinarily wants a higher level of emotional involvement and is more readily upset when she does not see it, thereby appearing more dependent. Yet she is more independent, in the important sense that it is easier for her to leave a relationship and to go on with her life. A typical man tries to appear independent but is more emotionally dependent in the important sense that he is less able to leave or to withstand the loss if the woman leaves. We masquerade as independent men and vulnerable women and hardly consider that we are designed to be otherwise.

Women *express* more distress about relationships, while men who experience distress ordinarily try to conceal it. When a relationship is in jeopardy, a woman is four or five times more likely to threaten suicide than a man, thereby obligating him to stay with her lest he be responsible for her death. Yet four times as many men as women actually commit suicide after failed relationships.[18]

The logic of genetic selection accounts for these perplexing traits. The woman who *appears* dependent obligates her mate to stay and provide for her, thus giving her children an advantage. She invites a man to feel responsible for her because she could not make it without him—or so it seems. And she invites the community to uphold her cause and pressure her fellow to do right by her. Yet when it is in her practical interest to leave, her relative independence makes it easier for her to do so than it would be for him. For men, genetic selection works the other way around. The man who *appears* strong and stable gives a woman confidence that he can support her, thereby increasing his chances of mating with her and producing offspring. Yet the sense of obligation that bonds him to his wife and children leaves him with less real independence than she has.

A parallel is seen in our romantic inclinations. Granted, women consume romantic fantasies, watch more romantic movies, now referred to as "chick flicks," and buy 98% of romance novels. Yet findings suggest that men accept the romantic myth that love conquers all and lasts forever, more so than women.[19] Men are more strongly attracted to their opposites than women are, and may report falling in love somewhat earlier in relationships.[20] And men may actually marry more for love, while women focus more on practical considerations.[21]

Just as an earlier generation resisted acknowledging that females ordinarily choose their mates, our own generation resists the finding that females are also the ones who ordinarily choose to dump their mates. Men want to see themselves in control, and women who see through the pretense may go along with it nonetheless to appear trustworthy and virtuous.

It is a poetic irony that the gender more interested in strictly casual sex with a variety of partners nonetheless bonds more solidly to a mate. It seems fair to say that men have more mixed feelings and more mixed up feelings in this area than do women. In spite of the wanderlust, some combination of obligation, love, social pressure, and the lack of emotional independence hold men more strongly in relationships.

♀
♁ In that many men commit more strongly than we typically realize, you might notice ways your fellow supports and provides for you. Shed a few of your insecurities and see if it makes sense to be more appreciative.

♂ So far as you are a typical fellow, realize that you are probably not as independent as you would imagine yourself to be. See your sense of obligation to a woman not as a weakness but as a strength that holds marriages together through hardships and provides security for children.

Why Women Are Less Satisfied in Marriages

Many of the same men who worry about getting married adjust well to being married, and most men anchor their personal identity in marriage and family. Over and over, findings confirm that married men are substantially healthier and happier than are men who are unmarried, divorced, or widowed.[22]

Women, more than men, are the ones who question the marriage arrangement and wonder if the deal is as good as it should be. Marriage for many women is a decidedly mixed blessing, scattering its joys and struggles about evenly and conferring overall neither advantage nor handicap. So we arrive at an observation that is a personal concern for some and of wider social concern as well: Women are generally less satisfied with their marriage and family life than are men.[23] Women, who have traditionally managed the relationships, are less satisfied living in them.

Why are wives less content than husbands? The usual explanations fall in two general categories—either women are oppressed and suffer from subordinate status in marriages, or women do more work and are exhausted from overworking. Each feels about right, but neither stands up to closer scrutiny. Women are considered formally subordinate to men, but by now we recognize the masquerade for what it is. We have seen how it all turns around when we look at who actually controls the arguments and who usually gives in. And while we hear that women do more than their share of the work, actual observations show that on average husbands work as much as wives. Women who hold jobs outside the home continue to do more of the housework and childcare than their husbands, which is unfair and should be corrected, but we have seen that overall men and women work about the same amount.

Try another explanation. Nature programs a woman, who traditionally required support, to question the commitment, to pick up
on any sign of wavering, to require compliance, and to be upset and
critical as a way of forcing the support she requires. So far as nature
commandeers her emotions to monitor his commitment, a woman has
the more emotionally wearing job. She may need a man to support her
and her children, but nature has not required her to idealize him or to
be wildly appreciative of him.

"When women are unhappy they usually think they need more love,
but the objective evidence suggests that they need more independence,"
notes Francesca Cancian. When men are unhappy, in contrast, they
usually think they need more success, but they need more time.[24] An
unhappy woman may feel that her relationship is making her unhappy,
and it is, but by fretting about it, she is also making herself unhappy. A
few observations suggest how this works. We have seen more than one
woman who was upset about a man who showed her too little attention,
who then separated, and found herself reasonably content with no
attention at all. It is not just that a woman needs more love from a man,
for if that were so she would feel worse, not better, when she loses the
little love she was getting. Her insecurities push for a stronger commitment, wearing her out, but she recovers when separation allows
her a respite.

In recommending more independence, Francesca Cancian means
that women need to be more comfortable with the imperfect relationships they have and to trust in their own survival with the man and
even, if it comes to that, without him.

Women may also be unintended casualties of our chivalrous
natures and customs, which sympathize with women and uphold their
complaints. A woman who *feels* she faces more than her fair share of
the sacrifices is apt to be unhappy about it, regardless of how fairly or
unfairly the sacrifices are actually shared. Questions of fairness are in
the eye of the beholder, of course, with few objective standards for
comparison. Even when men and women participate in the same
activities, we do not necessarily judge them the same. The same few
rounds of quick sex might leave him feeling great and her feeling used.
The objective criteria available, such as hours worked or financial

resources allocated, show men to be generally chivalrous and relationships to be reasonably fair.

Recognizing the balance might help women who want to feel more appreciative toward their mates and toward men in general. Recognizing their own substantial contributions might help men feel more adequate about themselves and about their involvement with wife and family, which would also be good.

Accomplished women and, "Why are there no good men out there?"
Wives working outside the home created some strains for traditional husbands a generation ago, but most men are reasonably well adjusted to it by now. The second income supplements the family finances, easing some of the pressures, and for many families it is now a necessity rather than an option. Wives work in about 60% of marriages in the United States.

What happens when the wife is more accomplished and earns significantly more money? Indeed, girls now outnumber boys in colleges, and 68% of freshman girls plan to get graduate degrees, compared to 65% of the boys.[25] It is surely a blessing for financially strapped men, but has a downside. When the man earns more money or at least as much, he provides an essential contribution that gives him a place in the family. When the woman earns more, what does the man provide that is so essential? Earning more does not reduce her emotional power. If anything, it makes a woman more powerful. So the high earning woman is the economic head of the family and the emotional powerhouse as well, while the man is neither. Is it so surprising that some men find that intimidating?

A sexual relationship is traditionally seen as a contribution a female provides for a male and for which she can expect to be compensated. We have seen that compensation for females is not merely a Western custom, but extends across cultures and is seen in many animal species as well. The expectation that men compensate women for romantic favors carries over into family finances. When the man earns more money, what he earns should be also hers simply because she is his wife. But when she earns more money, what she earns seems to remain hers until she chooses to share it with him.[26] How many of us feel that the man has earned a share of a woman's wealth simply because he shares her bed? So her higher earnings introduce an additional strain into the power balance, which is troublesome enough even under more traditional arrangements.

Women want men who can command resources, and highly successful women are no exception. Indeed, successful women are found to set higher expectations for a husband than less successful women.[27] Highly successful women who make more than $50,000 a year and hold professional positions are more apt to want mates who have professional degrees, high social status, high intelligence, and high incomes, than are less successful women. College women who expect higher earnings after college report a stronger preference for men with high earnings than do women who expect more modest incomes. Clearly, earning more money herself *raises* a woman's financial expectations for her husband, rather than lowering them.

How is a somewhat average man expected to compensate an exceptional woman who earns more? He might tend the children and do the housework, but is that enough? And would he be comfortable with himself doing that? A woman who wants to be compensated for her romantic favors is not overly inclined to pursue a man whom she must compensate.

A highly accomplished woman might lower her standards, choose a mate from among the less accomplished men available, make whatever allowances it takes to be together, and learn to love him. Or, she might go on daytime television and proclaim that there are no good men out there. Females are choosy, as Darwin observed a century and a half ago, and a fair number of highly successful women rate themselves above the available men. As more women earn high incomes, the chances diminish that they will find enough high income men to go around.

> I married beneath me. Of course, all women do.
>
> — Lady Astor

Numerous studies have found that the more a woman earns, especially in comparison to her husband, the higher the divorce rate.[28] Naturally, divorce rates are even higher in marriages where wives earn more than their husbands.[29, 30] In contrast, higher status men who earn more than their wives have more stable marriages. A financially successful man commands respect from his wife, who has practical reasons to stay. Note the contrast: Financially successful men have more stable marriages because they support their wives well, whereas financially successful women have less stable marriages, because they have the independence to leave.

Clearly, women who are socially and financially able to leave are more apt to do so. And so it has been across the ages.[31] In hunter-gatherer societies women often had independent resources, and divorce rates were relatively high. In early agricultural societies, in which men controlled the wealth of the land, marriages were stable and divorce was rare. Divorce began to rise during the industrial revolution, as women took jobs outside the home, and it continues to climb as women gain more financial independence.

A 1990s poll queried single Americans on whether they wanted to be married.[32] The vast majority of younger men and women—about 90%—looked forward to marriage. But within the critical 25 to 34 year old age span, 87% of single men but only 70% of single women wanted marriage. Thus twice as many women as men in this age group wanted to stay single. Even adjusting for more women in the population, that should have left enough men to go around. Ah, if only the women wanted to settle for the available men.

Of the reasonably attractive women over thirty who tell us there are no good men out there, all have one thing in common. Every one can acknowledge having had one or more men who wanted to marry her, but who was not up to her standards.

These contrasts between men and women run parallel to what we typically look for in a mate. Men tend to want sex while women are impressed by resources. Should it surprise us that men bond more strongly to the physical presence of a woman while women are more apt to follow the money?

Cஜ   ஜC

7.

Lopsided Conversations

Before marriage, a man declares that he would lay down his life
to serve you; after marriage,
he won't even lay down his newspaper to talk to you.

— Helen Rowland

Arriving home in the evening after work, we are all worn out and want to unwind and be ourselves. But we have different ideas of what that means.

Typical mismatch

Look here at an ordinary couple, after several years of marriage, as they try to unwind together after a long day. She wants to sit down together in the living room with some cheese, crackers and wine, and rehash the trials and triumphs and simple activities of the day. He wants to sit in front of the television with a cold beer and forget about the office and all that it requires of him. She wants to talk about who did what to whom, how everyone felt, her feelings about it, and what will happen next. He wants to watch the news or sports or just surf through the channels with his mind on cruise control, with no obligations.

These mismatched inclinations produce what has been called *the* conflict of modern marriages. One partner wants more interaction, more involvement, and more cooperation, while the other wants more space. So one criticizes and is upset, while the other retreats into silence. It is known as the "pursuer–distancer," as "demand–withdrawal," or "intrusion–rejection" pattern.[1] By whatever name, one chases and the other runs.

A woman typically wants more conversation, more openness, more sharing, more feelings, and more togetherness. In contrast, a man usually prefers some breathing space and the freedom to say what he wants or say nothing at all. He feels awkward in conversations about feelings and in emotional exchanges. So women are often the pursuers, while men are usually the distancers. The gender positions hold for perhaps two-thirds of relationships, but surely not all of them.

Pursuers and distancers bring out the worst in one another. Pursuers become upset, cold and critical when the mate is not as involved as they wish. Distancers remain passive and withdrawn, and escape conveniently into the long hours of a workaholic, the obsessions of a sports fanatic, the mindless comfort of a couch potato, or the welcome numbness of an alcoholic. The more one withdraws the harder the other pursues, and the harder one pursues the farther the other withdraws. The friction gives rise to typical feelings. She feels excluded; he feels intruded upon.

Chatty with chums

It has become something of a truism among relationship advice columnists and therapists as well that women are simply more talkative and that men have fewer words. Popular magazines have proposed that women use about twenty thousand words a day whereas men have about seven thousand, so that by the end of the day women want to continue talking whereas men have used up their quotas and are done with conversation for the day. It is a way of explaining to women readers why men do not talk more, so women will accept the arrangement rather than feel neglected and be unhappy.

Yet the folklore is just one segment of the story. Investigators led by Matthias Mehl of the University of Arizona followed almost four hundred college students and found no significant gender difference in how much these students talked. Some individuals were quite talkative and some were reserved, but the averages for the young men and the young women were the same—about sixteen thousand words a day.[2]

How should we reconcile the prevalent folklore with the University of Arizona finding? One possible explanation is that there is something in the average marital relationship that inclines women to continue conversing but has the opposite influence on men, inviting them to zip their mouths until they have something important enough to say. The tendency for women to dominate in arguments may contribute to the change.

Mate Training

Husbands are awkward things to deal with;
even keeping them in hot water won't make them tender.

— Mary Buckley

Women have traditionally required support and protection, and benefit most from civilized social conduct and are most readily harmed by its absence. If women are the socializing agents in any society, as Margaret Mead argues,[3] we would expect women to exert a strong influence on male conduct across cultures.

A woman marries a man in the hopes he will change,
and a man marries a woman in the hopes she will not change.
Ultimately, we are each disappointed.

— anonymous

Why use anger?

Women who want more communication are often upset and angry at their mates who fail to provide it. And being angry makes sense, of course, if only because it is the familiar response.

But step outside the familiar for a moment and ask an obvious question. Why use anger? It does not help a closed man feel safer about opening up. It does not help a cold man feel warmer. It does not help a hard man feel softer. As for coaxing someone to be emotionally closer to you, being upset is about as useful as a flame-thrower. Anger is better at pushing someone away than at inviting him closer. Its success rate is as close to total failure as you can possibly get.

So why is it our natural reaction? Remember that nature has programmed our emotions not for the intimacy we think we want, but for the propagation of our genes. As Darwin observed, emotions further human survival.[4] So nature arranges our emotions to support its own agenda. The aim of anger is not to promote conversation or to build intimacy, but to compel compliance and punish transgressions.

Being upset also pushes out the deadbeat who cannot be counted upon to provide and support. If he cannot hold up through a minor show of anger, a woman may be better off without him. And paradoxically, once we are paired up, the reassurance an angry individual requires can tighten the sense of obligation even while driving us farther apart.

> PMS is nature's way of ensuring
> that a man who stays to the next fertility cycle
> is truly committed.
>
> — anonymous

Women have traditionally looked to men for food and shelter, and warmth and communication appear to be newcomers in the marital equation. In divorce petitions in 1948, women mentioned non-support and heavy drinking as reasons for leaving, but not emotional reasons,[5] whereas by the 1980s their reasons had shifted to the currently familiar lack of communication and emotional incompatibilities. Unfortunately, human nature does not suddenly change to keep pace with our new interests. The anger and accusation that have been highly adaptive in pushing for financial support can be quite maladaptive in promoting our current interests in communication and intimacy. So here again, qualities that have been built into human nature from our ancestral past can become oddly maladaptive amid new requirements.

Say you love me!
Teenagers seem to have the same standard arguments about how often

the fellow calls and whether he is spending enough time with the girlfriend. If he does not call one night, or two in a row, she is worried and angry. She accuses him of not being interested in her anymore and not loving her. He replies that he just wanted to spend some time with his buddies, that she is making much ado about nothing, that he should not have to call her every night, and that he does love her. She is not so sure, and the two hammer at it for awhile and will do so again a few days later. She tells her friends that if he really loved her he would care enough to call. He tells his friends that she is high maintenance.

In our culture we even have an officially sanctioned day for ritual reassurance—Valentines day. Some men genuinely want to please the sweetheart and look forward to the romance, while others are merely fulfilling expectations. It is an open secret that men are obligated to buy the card and the flowers and chocolates and must do so. It is a day to express your love or face the consequences.

The woman who feels neglected might accuse her fellow of not really loving her, and he is expected to assure her that he does love her or face further accusations. What do we make of his reassurance? At that moment, he undoubtedly feels stressed. Realizing he is in trouble and unsure how to fix it, he could be feeling awkward and helpless, perhaps confused. He may be upset and angry at her for so much fussing over taking a night away from the phone. It could even cross his mind that she is more trouble than she is worth and that maybe he should try to get out of it.

Indeed, perhaps the one thing we know for sure that he is *not* feeling right then is an intense and overwhelming glow of love for her. Yet to resolve the argument and reconcile, he must reassure her that he loves her. The situation requires him to proclaim in a reasonably authentic manner the one feeling we can be sure at that moment that he is not feeling.

Squabbles as mate training

In a Monty Python skit, which we recreate loosely,[6] a sergeant major has his men lined up on the drill field. "Any of you have anything better to do than to march up and down this field all afternoon?" he demands menacingly. "Eh? Do you?"

One man, clearly intimidated, raises his hand. The sergeant turns to him, infuriated. "You think you have anything better to do than march up and down this field all afternoon? Eh?"

"Well, yes," the recruit stammers. "I thought I might practice the piano. If it's all right, that is, sergeant."

"All right, then," the sergeant barks. "Fall out." He turns again to the rest of the platoon, now furious. "Does anyone else have anything better to do than to march up and down this field all afternoon? Eh? Do you?"

A second recruit takes the chance. "I owe me mummy a letter home," he murmurs.

"All right, fall out," the sergeant commands. "Anyone else have anything better to do than to march up and down this field all afternoon?"

This time several men raise their hands, hesitantly. "There is a movie playing in town we thought we might like to see."

"All right, fall out!" the sergeant bellows. And so on it goes, until only the sergeant remains—who truly has nothing better to do than to march.

The skit is spoofing a serious situation. Normally, when your sergeant asks, you respond properly in compliance with expectations:

Sergeant: "Anyone have anything better to do than to march up and down this field all afternoon?"

Recruits, in unison: "No, sergeant!"

Any soldier who answers improperly would be ordered to fall out, dressed down in front of his unit, and then asked again. The sergeant is not asking for your feelings. The military requires compliance, and it is training the recruits to ignore their feelings and commit themselves to expectations. Soldiers conditioned to comply during interminable drills are more apt to comply later on when it matters, on the battlefield.

Look again at the man who must reassure his wife that he truly loves her. Who cares how he really feels? Nature wants to be sure he is fully committed, and so programs his wife to drill him. The man must ignore what he feels and meet expectations. The man who complies with expectations in these ritualistic confrontations is more apt to meet his responsibilities to his family later on when it really matters.

Perhaps understanding the meaning of these reassurance requirements can help us all walk through properly without taking them so
deathly seriously. See signs of reassurance as a normal facet of any
relationships.

♂ Reassurances comes in many forms. Be a good sport
about it and that may be reassuring in itself. Talk together about what counts as sufficient reassurance, and
see if you can find something you both agree upon.

Men who object can be put through the routine until they figure it
out or until everyone is exhausted by the squawking. The man who
feels more like swearing walks a tightrope. He knows better than to
fight with his woman and make matters worse, but he is unwilling to
reassure over and over which seems too much like a trained seal barking
on command.

Anger silences

A man who will not speak to his upset wife adds insult to injury, and the
woman may be so angry by now that she continues to accuse or actually
contradicts him when he does speak. She wants him to talk to her, but
she is too angry to listen to what he has to say.

As marriage therapists, we talk to the two of them together. We
mention that men often feel intimidated when their wives are so angry
and ask him if he feels intimidated. He says yes, he feels intimidated.
We ask him if he feels his wife listens when he does try to talk, or if she is
too angry to listen. He says she is always upset, and she jumps on him
for anything he says.

So long as someone is willing to listen, our formerly silent man is
surprisingly willing to talk about his feelings. Indeed, many men will
babble endlessly about themselves to anyone who seems genuinely
interested.

 If your husband hardly talks to you, ask yourself if you
hardly listen. You cannot express your anger and listen

at the same time. Ask yourself which is more important.

The Meaning of Romance

Women watch romantic movies, more so than men, read romance novels, and continue to peruse the various relationship advice columns. Women clearly consider romantic relationships as things to be fantasized, understood and managed, as an adventure with its thrills, chills, and spills, while men seem to want it to just work out smoothly and not cause them too many problems. Women are clearly far more comfortable with romance and its various flavors and nuances.

> In love women are professionals, men are amateurs.
>
> — Filmmaker François Truffaut

Signs of Love

Women more than men typically want words of love along with flowers, chocolates, romantic candlelight dinners, dancing, and the various other signs and symbols of a loving involvement. Women in happy marriages report more open expressions of love than those in unhappy marriages, which should not surprise anyone.[7]

Men are typically less interested in these traditional features of romance, meaning that some tension is almost inevitable and that women will find themselves having to coax men to be more romantic. Obviously, these romantic gestures mean different things for women than they do for men, and for the familiar reasons.

Insuring a commitment is especially important for women, in that females invest more in producing and in nurturing a child. Women stand to benefit substantially from the continuing support a man might provide but are left in the lurch by the man who fails to provide. Since much of the required support is far in the future, women must rely on signs which indicate that the man is good for the commitment. Words of love and romantic gestures are traditional signs of commitment, and nature has programmed these to be more important to women than to men.

What men see as love

A man does not ordinarily pester his wife or sweetheart for expressions of love and endearment. Indeed, he may not ask his mate even a single question about how much she loves him or even about whether or not she loves him at all. As long as a woman is being affectionate and sexually intimate with him and no one else, he feels she is giving herself to him and that she loves him. If she is not allowing intimacies, he may wonder whether she loves him and may wonder if she is with someone else. He may argue that if she really loved him she would want to have sex with him, and thereby try to pressure her into it, which most of us would consider underhanded and objectionable. Yet it is not the pledge of undying love but the sex itself which he finds reassuring.

Why the difference? Women benefit genetically from a committed relationship and so are often pleased with the romance, the pro-clamations, and the snuggling that show commitment. Men benefit genetically from sexual favors, in casual relations as well as committed ones, and so are pleased by the sexual intimacies that pass along their genes.

An insecure fellow is not ordinarily looking for words of love. Perhaps he is afraid that his woman is cheating on him, and he accuses her of flirting or seeing someone else or merely wanting to see someone else, and he continues on and on in spite of her denials. The accusations serve to intimidate and control, and she either complies with his demands or ducks out and goes on without him.

A boy can ask his friends whether a girl likes him to figure out whether he should talk to her or take the chance and ask her out. He might ask a girl if she loves him if he is trying to figure out whether to go steady with her or whether he should ask her to marry him. Yet the average man does not ask a woman if she loves him just to reassure himself that she is there for him.

Feeling it and meaning it

Do you love someone? Does your someone love you in return? How do you figure it out?

The love words have aspects of "feeling it" and aspects of "meaning it." You can think of love as a feeling or as a commitment.[8] In the first case you want to say what you feel, and in the second case you should mean what you say.

When love refers to a feeling, it means you have an infatuation, a longing, a rush or a sense of comfort with somebody. When love refers to a commitment, it means you obligate yourself to continue with the relationship and to take care of the one you love.

So, how do you know if it is love? If it is a feeling, you look to your inner experience to see if the feelings are on or off. So far as it is a commitment, you ask whether you are willing to be there for your beloved. Obviously, in our conversations about love, we slide between the feeling it and the meaning it aspects of the word.

Words of love tend to obligate men more than women, as do relationships generally. The man who says "I love you" should be committing himself to continue in a relationship, telling his sweetie that she can count on him. So if he bails out on her he can be accused of breaking a promise and not meaning what he has said. When a woman says "I love you," she may be giving a compliment or obligating her partner to love her in return, but she may be only modestly committing herself. If her feelings change and she bails out on him, family and friends do not hold her to her word and try to force her to continue the courtship that she no longer desires. Most women learn to avoid talking about love too early in a relationship, to avoid introducing an obligation that may scare a man off.

Women are more comfortable with the world of romance while men are more often tangled up in concerns about obligation. We might easily surmise that women are more comfortable with words of love because they can more easily experience the feeling without having to obligate themselves to a commitment.

Some men manage to duck the usual association of love with obligation, and can proclaim their love at considerable length to whoever arouses their feelings. When the feeling is gone, the fellow too is gone. The woman is left to question how the man could have loved her in the first place if he could leave so easily. She concludes that he did not really mean what he said, and in a sense she is right. He felt an attraction for her and called it love, but he did not mean he was committed to her.

Perhaps this is helpful to women who want more talk about love. Would you want a man who talks freely about the love he experiences but does not consider it a commitment once the rush is over? Is his love not superficial or false?

Many men do not always bond more strongly, or hardly bond at all, which should go without saying. Women with such men must be quite clear about what they want and sometimes forceful for a relationship to stay on course.

Manly ways

Men have other reasons for steering clear of the love words. To the sex that is fond of rugged masculine words like "damn" and "hell," the love words sound squishy soft. Is it possible to combine the two into some sort of rugged masculine proclamation of affection? Could you say, "Damn, I love you, woman!"? How many women would accept it? And what about the illusion of independence, which men cherish? Since love bonds, a man expressing his love is admitting that he is not as independent as he would wish to believe.

A man tends to see marriage as a tremendous additional responsibility, even today when his wife might earn an equal salary. The unfortunate consequence is that a man who communicates openly before marriage may clam up and stop talking altogether under the burden of the additional responsibility, leaving his new wife wondering whatever happened. How do we bridge these differences?

♀ Interpret the commitment itself as a sign of love. The everyday activities of life together are all statements of involvement, so long as we do them joyously and not begrudgingly.

♂ You need not retreat into silence. Talk about what being together means to you, in whatever terms you wish. Or you might try being more comfortable with conventional signs of affection. Think of flowers and sweet nothings not as silly romanticism, but as a step in mastering the masculine position in a relationship.

Overly sensitive vs. clueless

"Honey, we need to talk about where we are going with our relationship." Sound familiar? It is almost invariably the woman who initiates these conversations while the man tries to avoid them. She may see it as a chance to get closer, although it serves not to get closer but to resolve her sense of insecurity. He sees it as intimate persecution.

Why is a woman so concerned about how her man feels? Since she traditionally has had to rely on a man for support, being sensitive to his moods and feelings allows her to make adjustments as required. Such sensitivity confers a survival advantage, and it has been passed to the next generation. Nature programs a woman's feelings to monitor a man's commitment.

When one member of a pair is ready to leave and the other has not had the slightest idea anything is wrong, it is typically the woman who is on her way out and the man who is clueless. A woman will almost always know when something is wrong, and she will be upset and asking questions. As wives are upset more often than men find comfortable, many men learn to live with the emotional turbulence by fulfilling their responsibilities and trying not to take the emotions too seriously. The husbands say, "Yeah, I knew we had some problems. Everyone does. She was upset sometimes. But I had no idea it was anything so serious." Her announcement that she is leaving comes as a bolt out of the blue.

Intimacy vs. our wiring

Realize that emotions have their own agendas and serve purposes that are not necessarily our purposes. In addition to forcing a commitment, being upset also pushes the man away from the cozy world of love and out into the world of accomplishment. By making it uncomfortable at home, an upset woman pressures a man to take on the hardships of long days in the fields, the risks of the hunt, or the dangers of battle. Where do we go with these entangling communications?

 To nurture closeness, you will need to tolerate some insecurity, rather than interrogate your fellow to force him into reassuring you.

Realize that some emotional conflicts are just gender rituals, and do not take them so personally.

Sometimes just recognizing our differences can suffice. Deborah Tannen writes of a couple who had a wonderful first night together and were continuing with a special breakfast when he opened his newspaper.[9] Ordinarily, she would have felt taken for granted and would have fussed at him. But having read that men can feel intimate with less conversation, she kept the faith and the relationship stayed on course. Of course, nature did not program her to take a chance on it. What if he really was taking her for granted?

> In the sex war thoughtlessness is the weapon of the male,
> vindictiveness of the female.
>
> — Cyril Connolly

A wife may gauge her relationship as much on what her mate says to her as on what he does for her. Indications are that a woman is happiest when her husband *says* he loves her, while a man wants his wife to *do* things that show love.[10]

To avoid unnecessary hazing, express your love clearly and often enough that your wife can feel secure. If she must be sure about your love, how many ways can you tell her how much she means to you? You will be more convincing, and surely more relaxed, if you do it before she is upset enough to try to force you to do it.

Information talk vs. feelings talk

Who talks more depends somewhat on the topic and the situation. Men offer more information about things, while females speak more about personal feelings and social relations.[11] Men talk at length about sports, politics, society, finances, how things work—and almost anything in which one might show himself informed and thoughtful. Women talk freely about more personal subjects—what other people are doing, saying and feeling, and about who is justified and who is wrong.

When women complain that men do not talk enough, they mean that men do not talk to them enough about feelings and personal concerns. The same men who are so present in public conversations seem to vanish in the personal arena.

More vs. Better Communication

Of several hundred psychiatrists asked to list the major reasons that marriages fail, an impressive 45 percent said that the primary cause is the husband's failure to communicate his feelings.[12] Only 9 percent blamed sexual incompatibility. So the husbands were faulted for insufficient communication, not the wives for expecting too much of it. This is probably typical of the helping professions, where we value communication and prescribe more of it to fix relationships.

Many people believe that simply expressing feelings promotes marital satisfaction. A survey of 280 unmarried undergraduate students found that 75 percent agreed that increased self-expression, whether warm or angry, enhances marital satisfaction for both partners.[13] Watch out! People who believe that can express the whole array of angry feelings and be self-righteous about it, shredding important relationships while imagining themselves innocent of any wrongdoing.

Communication is important, but it is not *how much* we communicate that contributes to the quality of a marriage. A vast array of research finds no strong connection between the amount of communication and the level of satisfaction in a relationship, and many studies find no connection at all. We see solid marriages in which relatively few words are spoken, and rocky marriages in which constant explosions of antagonistic feelings perpetuate the animosities.

One group of investigators observed the number of interactions between partners over the course of their relationships.[14] Interestingly, the highest levels of communication were found at the beginning and the end of a relationship. On the second date, when we are just getting interesting, we reveal ourselves and try to find out about each other—

our likes and dislikes, our plans, what sorts of families we have, and so on. And the final year of a failing marriage we riddle one another with recrimination:

> SHE: "If you had half as much interest in me as you had in your damned career, maybe you would show some of it before we get to the bedroom!"

> HE: "Of course Madam has to be courted for hours and hours to be properly prepared, especially when she is not particularly fond of the man she is with."

A great deal of communication usually signals that something is changing in a relationship, for better or for worse. Communication can wound as easily as it can heal, and it can create misunderstandings as easily as it can clear them up. It can push us apart and prod us to dig in our heels as easily as it can resolve concerns and bring us closer. The good communication that benefits a marriage is not just clearly spoken or honest to a fault. It reflects consideration of each other, and it attempts to build bridges across our differences.

In the handful of truly vital marriages, the men are every bit as open in talking about themselves as are the women.[15] These happily married men tell about their dreams and aspirations, their weaknesses and dissatisfactions with themselves, and so on, and feel their wives understand. Even men in average marriages rely upon their wives to be their best friends, and men who are not close to their wives risk being isolated and lonely.

Given how much women push for more communication, you might think women are the only ones to benefit from it. Yet men benefit from it every bit as much.

 Open communication may be to your own advantage. If you do not like the topics your wife suggests, set your own agenda.

♀ You have a fresh argument here for more communication. Tell your man that research says it will be good for him and that he will feel isolated and unhappy without it. Then be open to what he wants to talk about.

CR SO

8.

Cautious Silence

The change women want most
is for men to talk about their feelings,
and the change men want most is to be understood
without having to talk about their feelings.

— Michael McGill

The same silence that women find so frustrating can be a perversely rational solution for the addled fellow in a confusing situation. He remains a mystery, because of his silence, to the woman in his life, of course, but often to himself as well. We look to understand his confusion and also silence as a countermeasure.

Upset

Anger and tears may produce an odd and often confusing challenge. "Being upset" usually refers to a combination of being hurt and also angry at whoever hurt you. Perhaps the two are logical companions in all of us. But a woman who is angry *shows* hurt much more than a man, while the usual posture among men is to underplay the hurt and show only the anger. It is the combination of hurt and anger together that creates a double bind and emotional gridlock.

A woman who is simply hurt invites a man to try to comfort and protect her, whereas one who is straightforwardly angry invites him to fight against her. But how does a man relate to a woman who is hurt *and* angry? He cannot simply support her, because she is attacking him, but he cannot openly fight her, because she is so hurt. Facing two poor choices, he is also unable to understand his confusion or comment on it.

The hurt and anger together create what is referred to as a double bind, meaning a choice between two wrong alternatives. The usual reaction to a double bind is the emotional withdrawal that we have come to expect of men when women are upset. While few men have heard of the double bind, most men understand the confusion. Many men realize that they do not win an argument when the wife is upset and so fall silent to avoid provoking further hurt and anger.

To most women, the silence is extraordinarily frustrating. A woman interprets the silence as a refusal to take her seriously and an unwillingness to be involved. It further upsets her and she pushes him harder, causing him to withdraw farther, thus forming a vicious cycle.

This double bind provides women a tactical power advantage, but at a price. Nature hands the upset woman sufficient power to intimidate her noncompliant mate, and in the process blindly sacrifices the intimacy she cherishes. We suspect that many women are more interested in the companionship than in the tactical advantage.

You can improve the situation some by clearly separating your hurt from your anger. If you are sad and hurt and want support from your mate, you should make it crystal clear that you are not angry at him. Otherwise, he will feel he is being blamed for something.

On the night she and her fellow got engaged, a young woman got her feelings hurt over a joke made about being married, and she began to cry. He told her he could not stand to see a woman cry and went into the next room and sat down by himself. Sound familiar? She followed him in and sat down on his lap. She told him she was not mad at him but was just hurt, and asked him to hold her while she cried, which he did. She told him she loved him very much and did not ever want to be without him. Then he cried. Some years later she told us that he is still nervous when she cries, but he no longer tries to flee. She still tells him to hold her, which he always does, and they talk it through.

♀ Try asking your husband to hold you the next time you get your feelings hurt. Most men are willing to try to be helpful, so long as you seem friendly. Tell him it feels good to be close to him when you are hurt. Make it a success experience for him, and he will be closer to you the next time.

♂ Recognize that sadness, like anger, is not nearly as serious as most men assume. Look to understand the pain behind the tears. You might allow yourself even to experience some of it yourself. The tragedies of life are part of the human experience, to be shared with someone you love.

Why men conceal weaknesses

It is well known that men do not usually reveal personal weaknesses. Passed over for a promotion and deeply troubled about it, the average man will be ashamed to tell his wife and may avoid mentioning it at all. Robert Fulghum writes of a doctor who had terminal cancer but hid it from his wife and family. When he died, they were angry about not getting to say good-bye to him. As in hide-and-seek, you can hide so well that everyone gives up looking for you, and you are left alone. "Get found, kid!" Fulghum advises.[1]

As a therapist, I (Driscoll) talk openly about my weaknesses and failings to set the tone and to explore how personal issues might be resolved. Yet outside of my profession, I do not reveal my weaknesses much more than other men do, and I can find it terribly embarrassing when they show. Why the difference? When a therapist shares his weaknesses, it is as a way of providing good therapy—that is, of being strong.

When I played soccer, I considered the fellows on my team friends. But I would not expect any one of them to announce it if he were failing in business, if his wife were running around with another man, or if he found out he had terminal cancer. When I was younger, I occasionally mouthed off too much which, in addition to being a mediocre player, kept me off of a team I would have wanted to play on. When I got the bad news, I felt a searing sense of shame rush all the way through me. It was about a year before I mustered the grit to tell my wife about it. Being a mediocre player never bothered me, but I felt my breach of sports etiquette showed a significant personal weakness.

Society expects men to be strong, of course, but that does not explain why so many men take it so deadly seriously. Did anyone ever tell me that if and when I mess up and lose face, I should experience intense, searing shame and not tell anyone? If so, I don't remember it.

Try another explanation. Traditionally, women are attracted to men with strength and position, who can be expected to support a family, while men look for women who are young and pretty. Evolutionary psychologist David Buss found that in each of 37 cultures he examined, females place more emphasis on financial prospects in selecting a mate than do males.[2] Women are turned off by qualities suggesting an inability to produce, such as lack of ambition or lack of education.[3] In sizing up a man, it is not unusual for women to talk openly about his prospects as a provider. When Henry Kissinger said that power is the only real aphrodisiac, he hit close to the mark. Over the ages, the man who ranks high among other men could be expected to bring home his share of the haul and take good care of his mate. Low-status males with known weaknesses were judged unsuitable as providers and were chosen last or did not mate at all.

A good case can be made that it is quite the same today even when so many women must work to contribute to the family income.[4] While women with careers usually choose mates for personal compatibility, they typically choose from men who are ambitious and seem to be going somewhere, not from the failures and bums. Research indicates that men who reveal insecurities too soon or too often are regarded by women (and by men as well) as being "too feminine" and "poorly adjusted."[5] Thus, oddly, the openness that a woman wants in a man can reduce his status and ruin his chances with her. Now as in ages past, the selection process weeds out the man who naively reveals his weaknesses. The man who conceals his failures is more successful in wooing a mate, and the inclination to be ashamed of weakness is passed along to successive generations of men.

Can you imagine a woman attracted to weakness instead of

strength? It might look like this:

HE: I found out today I was passed over for a promotion again. Smith got it. The boss said if my production doesn't improve, I will be out of a job.

SHE: Oh, you adorable loser! You make me hot! Help me out of these fashionable clothes and take me to heaven.

Sure, it might happen—about once in a blue moon. Just as success instills confidence, weakness and failure introduce doubt about a viable future together.

So if a man is to mate and his genes to continue, it is in his interest to appear to be doing well and to conceal any failures and weaknesses which might disqualify him. Nature programs a man to strive for power and to conceal his losses as best he can. Here, male interest and female interest collide. It is in a woman's interest to find out as much as she can about a prospect before she hitches her wagon to his star.[6] So while he is programmed to show his strengths and conceal flaws that would make him less marketable, she wants the open communication and personal disclosure that allows her to size up her man, know him intimately, and be comfortable with him.

Propriety and censorship

A woman who wants a man to talk freely may assume quite incorrectly that she will like hearing about whatever he is thinking. Most women would be in for an unpleasant surprise or two.[7] The sort of raunchy conversation that adolescent boys enjoy with one another is judged to be crude, lewd, rude, and socially unacceptable in front of females. Mothers are highly offended by unrefined adolescent male patter, and they censure boys who talk too openly, and fathers ordinarily support them. Teenage boys who talk freely about their sexual thoughts and feelings with the fellows learn to clean up their acts in mixed company. Women censure offensive male language, and males learn to censor themselves to get along.

While a man may find conversation between females trivial and boring, a woman can find stock male language crude and offensive. Neither gender will be pleased by how the other judges it, but our reactions are not weighted evenly. When a man offends a woman, he is judged socially inappropriate and feels ashamed. Typically, he resolves to be more careful about what he says in mixed company. When a woman hears that her small talk bores a man, she is offended, and she lets him know he was rude and insensitive. He will add the item to his list of what he is not supposed to reveal.

Note the asymmetry. When a man makes critical judgments about female conversation, women judge back, and the man hushes. When a woman is critical of male conversation, men hush or take their conversation elsewhere. The outcome in either case is that a man learns to be careful about expressing himself on gender-sensitive issues.

Men sometimes complain that the rules are continually changing and that they never know when they will be censured. Some women are now offended by being called "ladies," while others consider it properly respectful. Using the generic "he" and "his" to refer to an individual of unspecified sex is now judged sexist, while a generation ago it was considered proper grammar. Manners and etiquette, in the best sense, are the rules that help us live together more comfortably and avoid unnecessary friction. In their practical implementation, manners often mean doing what pleases women and avoiding what offends them. Women judge men on their good manners or lack thereof, and men pick up the cues. Men suppress the sort of conversation that women judge improper, or they conduct it away from women.

We can hardly imagine a civilization in which males give voice to anything that wanders through their minds and women accept it without comment. Some censorship is required for comfort and reasonable propriety, and each new couple must establish its own boundaries.

She talks—he scans, censors, and presents himself

Talking about oneself requires considerably more concentration for a man than it does for a woman. A woman who talks about herself has only to note her thoughts and feelings and express them as they come to mind. It sounds effortless, and often it is. A man who talks about himself must orchestrate an impromptu performance. He must scan his thoughts and feelings; select those that are interesting and sound suitably manly; organize and present them in a sincere manner, but without falsehoods or exaggerations that might expose him as a fraud, while censoring anything which could reveal weaknesses or might offend. He works to appear open and comfortable with himself while conscientiously avoiding the sort of mistakes that would cause him to lose standing. So even a few comments about himself can require considerable concentration. Not surprisingly, men who converse all day at work are not always so interested in continuing it with the wife at home.

Some men seem not to know their own feelings at the time but then figure them out two days or two weeks later. "Do you miss me?" "Are you worried about your job?" "Do you want to have another baby?" To a man, each of these questions is a chance to mess up. Should he reveal an emotional weakness? Should he acknowledge his uncertainty about his job and worry her? Should he talk about the financial stress of another child and allow her to think he cannot handle it? Something inside him censors his feelings, even from himself, until he has had some time to think about the situation, weigh it all out, and arrive at an acceptable statement. If this does not induce men to be more open, or incline women to accept a closed-off man, it does explain our differences.

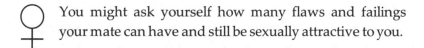

♀ You might ask yourself how many flaws and failings your mate can have and still be sexually attractive to you.

♂ Ask yourself how attractive your wife would find you if your career was unraveling around you. Would she still accept you after a significant reversal? Are you giving her enough credit? And could you accept yourself?

Actually, women are not turned off by *all* weaknesses. While women are generally repelled by a weakness for alcohol or drugs, and any weakness of mind, body or character that makes a man a poor provider, she can feel secure with a man who has a weakness for her. She may be thrilled by the man who has to be close to her and hold onto her, who loves her and feels her love for him, and who would be totally lost without her. Feeling needed helps provide the sense of security that success alone cannot provide.

♂ If you have a soft place in your heart for your wife, by all means share it! It may not be the easiest thing to talk about, but it gets you farther than almost anything else you can share.

Men in truly vital relationships can be quite open about their dreams and failures and expect their wives to understand. A man who can openly share his failings with his wife has an unusual amount of trust in her and in himself, which can carry him through a few hard times.

Countermeasures

The reasons for silence range from the apparently innocent confusion and stress, through passive resistance as an assertion of independence, to passive aggression and sulking as a payback for grievances. The confused are innocent but weak, the passively resistant exercise some control, and the sulkers are angry and punitive while trying to conceal it. All fall short of our reasonable expectation of active participation in a relationship.

So which is it? Is the quiet fellow stressed, resistant, or angry? It is usually worth it for a woman to puzzle out which it is, and it is worth it for the fellow as well, who may not know which it is himself.

The man who is proclaiming his independence could be clearer about what he is doing and try to negotiate a better settlement. If he is not participating because the wife interrupts him, he should state his case, and see if the two can agree for him to involve himself more while she tries to interrupt less.

One who sulks is saying "Look how miserable and angry you have made me," and he continues to be miserable as a testament to how badly he was treated. One who sulks typically avoids saying just what his partner did that was so wrong, figuring either that she already knows or should know or that if she does not know he will not tell her and thereby make it too easy for her. Sulking thus involves a sense of being unfairly treated; anger and an impulse to lash back; a wariness of open confrontation; misery and anger as a way to cast blame; and perhaps some secret satisfaction in not saying what one is so troubled by. Women sulk too, of course, although men seem to do more of it. Sulking is ordinarily a tactic of the more intimidated, while the more confident individuals express anger more openly.

One who sulks can take a significant step out of it by just saying what he is doing. So the fellow might tell his wife "You yell at me in front of the kids, so I am being miserable, to show you how miserable you have made me, and I may continue to be miserable until you fix it." Once he openly exposes himself, he spoils his little ruse and is less apt to continue with it.

Bridging the differences

Indications are that women experience emotions more intensely and are more emotionally volatile than men. Research notes that women report more negative and troublesome feelings than men, but also more joyous and positive feelings as well.[8] So part of why women talk about their feelings is that women have more feelings to talk about.

Men can see women as too emotional and too bound up by their feelings, while women can see men as too unfeeling or too closed off from their feelings. Having more feelings or fewer feelings is neither good nor bad—both contribute to the richness of our lives.

Will men lose interest in sports and acquire a liking for long conversations about love and other sensitive feelings? Probably not. Will women want to talk mainly about things instead of about people? No, probably not.

How do we bridge our contrasting preferences for feelings talk? For starters, we might distinguish between our initial differences and the problems that arise from our responses to those differences. Women who are upset with their husbands for not talking are inadvertently creating further silence. Men who withdraw because their wives are upset are inadvertently creating more resentment.

Those who frequently feel upset should realize that your own feelings are driving your husband farther away from you.

Suppose a woman suggests talking about her relationship. Her husband gives her that "Oh no, here we go again" expression, and glances around for the nearest exit. Instead of being exasperated, she tries to hear what he feels.

"You're not looking forward to this?" she suggests.

"Well, no," he answers.

"Afraid I'm going to be cross with you?"

"I guess I just never know what to say."

Of course he suspects that she will be cross with him, if that has been her pattern. She addresses his concern: "I am not annoyed or anything. I just have some things I need to talk about."

 Try to understand the problems instead of being upset about them. Your otherwise reserved husband will be more willing to open up.

A woman who wants to be heard does not simply vanish because her husband does not want to listen. As long as she wants a relationship with him and not an outside affair, he is what she has available. The conversation he walked away from today will still be waiting for him tomorrow.

 Those who withdraw when feeling trapped should recognize by now that you are inviting further pursuit.

Those who withdraw might look at why they do so. Is your wife so hard to talk to? Are you confused or intimidated by her seemingly relentless questions, or by her moodiness?

♂ Can you tell her how it feels? If you feel too stressed and cannot manage an argument, you might as well say so! "When you're upset at me, I get tense inside. You're better at arguing than I am, so you usually have the last word."

If a man manages to say all that, will his wife listen and understand? If so, they are beginning to communicate. But what if she feels he is blaming her and gets angrier? Might he do better to remain silent?

When silence means no preference

Living with a partner who does not express preferences can be confusing. The upside is that you get to have everything your way. The downside is that you make every choice alone and can feel like you are living with your own shadow.

A young woman we counseled wondered if her fiancé was really as involved as he should be. He would never say what he wanted to do, which show he wanted to see, where he wanted to eat. Whatever she wanted was fine with him. With friends, he was always pleasant but had little to say. He was in upper management and worked a full eighty hours a week, every week. Most of his free hours he spent with her. He was generous and bought her anything she wanted.

What *was* wrong with him? As we talked, it became clear that he was too worn out to find much happiness in anything he might do. Yet he was pleased being with her while she was happy, and it pleased him to make her happy. The best he could manage was a vicarious pleasure, in loving a woman who herself loved life.

Understanding her fiancé helped her realize that she was truly special to him, in spite of his silence. The two of them together chose to accept the situation and to work around it, for the time, as he was doing well in the job and could not reschedule his hours. We would hope that his long-range plans included a job change.

 Realize that the man who does not express an opinion is not necessarily trying to withhold himself. He may be trying to be considerate or may not have an opinion. Or, as in the case above, he may find more satisfaction in doing what you want.

♂ Realize that indifference can be maddening. If you do not have a strong preference where to eat, then offer whatever slight preference you have. If you mainly just want your mate to be happy, tell her that is what you want. And if it would make her happy for you to chose where to eat, by all means do so.

My (Driscoll's) own solution is to state my preference, and then quickly go along with whatever everybody else wants.

Some preferences are simply preferences

When we are first in love, we want to do the same things. Men are fascinated talking to their sweethearts, hours and hours on end, and go willingly to the theater, out to dinner, and maybe even dancing. Believe it or not, some men even volunteer to go shopping with their girlfriends. Women like watching football, riding on the back of the motorcycle, even camping in the rugged outdoors miles from any facilities. The truth is that in the haze of love, we will do almost anything that the other wants to do and will love it, simply because we want to be together.

After the rush subsides, this changes. We again care about the activities themselves, at least as much as doing things together. Our individual inclinations reassert themselves. Those who want more involvement sometimes interpret this to mean that the partner does not care.

♀ Ask yourself if you are willing to do what he wants to do. Would he welcome you along with his beer and football buddies? Love is as much about respecting another's preferences as about remaking them to match your own.

♂ If you loved being more involved before you married, realize that you have changed. What would it take to enjoy doing some of the things you did together before you married?

Evolution could have easily shaped our preferences for certain activities. Men seem to love sports more than women do. Sports, as recreational combat, are about winning and losing and the power and tactics by which we might prevail. Men, of course, have always had to judge the strength of competing groups to figure how to make the best alliances and stay with the winners. Football involves powerful men in brutal clashes over yardage, loosely paralleling the strictly male practice of attacking or defending geographic territory. A wide range of sports including basketball, soccer and golf, involve placing a projectile on a target, paralleling the activity of early hunters (who were almost always men).[9]

Shopping involves selecting needed items and bringing them back home, loosely paralleling the gathering activities of women in hunter-gatherer cultures. And conversing about personal matters helps women in their traditional job of staying abreast of relationships.

Marriage provides us with an inordinate amount of free time together that we did not have before marriage. Even the most accomplished conversationalists can occasionally run out of things to say.

We might communicate some tolerance for the natural limitations of human nature.

CR SO

9.

Expressers and Fixers

If women resent men's tendency to offer solutions to problems,
men complain about women's refusal to take action
to solve the problems they complain about.

— Deborah Tannen

Men and women deal with personal problems in sharply contrasting
ways. Women tend to share their troubles more freely and openly,
while men tend to keep their problems very much to themselves.

In so doing we collude to create the impression that women are
more fragile, weaker, and surely more insecure than men. The impression is but another illusion, of course, in the marvelous masquerade.
A greater tendency to share weakness and insecurities should not
be misconstrued to mean that women are therefore weaker or more
insecure. It only means that women are more open about their vulner-
abilities, while men are more private about them.

Reactions

Men and women also differ in how we respond to the personal
problems of others. Women try to empathize with one another, expressing sympathy and encouraging each other to continue talking
about the problems. Women often share something similar from their

own experiences, suggesting that while life can be rough, we are all in it together. Men usually try to fix the problem, either by providing information or by conveying that it is not so important. At the extremes, same gender conversations can produce unintended humor.

Suppose an adolescent girl complains to her friends about her appearance:

ADOLESCENT GIRL: "I'm gaining too much weight. I look fat in this dress."

GIRLFRIEND: "I know just what you mean. I have a whole closet of clothes that I can never wear anymore, because they make me look just awful."

2ND GIRLFRIEND (who weighs 110 pounds but joins in anyway): "I have to watch everything I eat or I will blow up like a blimp."

The message is that "I understand—I'm just like you, you're just like me, we are in it together." The aim is to find common ground and to give voice to the common experience.

A fellow complaining to his buddies about his appearance would be met with a very different response:

ADOLESCENT BOY: "I'm thin as a rail. I have no muscles."

GUY FRIEND: "What do you mean, man? You look fine."

2ND GUY (ribbing him): "You do look thin as a toothpick. Hey man, you need to pump a little iron before you blow away somewhere and I can't find you. Then who am I going to get to give me a ride home?"

The message is, "Toughen up, it's not so bad, joke it off. And if something is wrong, stop complaining and go fix it." Here the insecurity itself is the problem and the friend is trying to fix it so his companion will operate properly again, meaning that he will operate confidently. The aim among fellows is to support morale, maintain group solidarity, and get on with the common activities.

Same-gender groups fall naturally into gender-appropriate practices and socialize their members in these practices. Females are expected to tell their personal secrets, and those who do not are considered aloof and remain outsiders. Males are expected to be tough, and those who show weakness are in for some ribbing. Research on friendship in America shows that men tend to form friendships based on shared activities and do not reveal personal weakness, while women form friendships based on sharing feelings and can usually name a best friend.[1]

Females share their troubles, as Deborah Tannen suggests, to establish a personal connection, to maintain intimacy, and to avoid appearing aloof. Males rib one another not to create distance, but as a sign of respect. The message is, "Your problems are not so serious and you are strong enough to benefit from my ribbing."[2]

In cross-gender relationships, we continue in the gender-typical ways. Females want to express feelings, while males try to fix whatever is wrong. In the best of all possible worlds, when everything goes smoothly, expressers and fixers complement each other. A woman expresses a problem, inviting involvement and support, and a man understands the problem and suggests a practical solution. She appreciates what he does to help, and he feels noble for being so helpful. Unfortunately, few interactions go so smoothly.

Conversing About Personal Problems

Many personal problems cannot be fixed by simple reassurance or straightforward suggestions. The quick fix is seldom a fix at all, as in the following exchange:

SHE: "I have no real friends."
HE: "Lots of people like you. But if you feel that way, you could get out and meet more people."
SHE: "What do you care, anyway?"

Ordinarily, those who express their worries want first to be understood and to feel that they are being taken seriously, and only then to consider a solution. So the fellow here seems to fail to understand the seriousness of her feelings, and she judges him unconcerned and is unwilling to listen to his solution. Anyone who provides a quick and easy answer has overlooked this initial requirement, and his wonderful suggestions will fall on deaf ears. The man who gives the fast answer seems to have not heard the full problem and the depth of pain. Inadvertently, he is also presenting himself as wiser and thus superior, merely by being sure of the answer while she has no clue. So his unintended message is, "You cannot figure out your problems, although you have struggled with them, but I can quickly see what you need to do to fix everything."

It is not that you cannot reassure or that you cannot offer suggestions. But you cannot offer them right off, as men often try to do, to just fix the problem and get on with other things. It is a matter of sequencing.

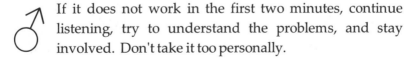 How do you show that you are listening? One of the best ways is to actively reflect what your partner is saying before you go on to comment upon it. Then see if you can offer a solution and have it accepted.

SHE: "I have no real friends."

HE: "You feel nobody likes you?"
Or, "You feel you have acquaintances, but not real friends?"
Or, "Are you feeling lonely?"

Any of these might be the feeling. She will tell you whether you hit it, and clarify it further.

If it does not work in the first two minutes, continue listening, try to understand the problems, and stay involved. Don't take it too personally.

The flip side here is that women who respect and appreciate their husbands are more apt to consider their suggestions, while women who are fighting for control are unlikely to accept suggestions under any conditions whatsoever.

 If you want your husband to be involved in your concerns, try to find something in what he says that you can accept or agree with or find helpful in some way.

Men take complaints seriously

Almost any man whose wife is upset almost invariably feels stressed about the situation and pressured to fix whatever is wrong. When the problem does not bow to an easy solution, the pressure builds.

SHE: "I am really tired of this house and all the ratty furniture. Nothing ever gets fixed. I am ashamed to have guests over."

He (angrily): "We moved here because this is what you said you wanted."

The man here takes her being upset as an accusation that he is not providing for her sufficiently, and he counters by blaming it on her own foolish choices. Here his stress translates directly to anger. He has not told her what is stressing him, and she will not understand why he is angry at her. A man whose wife is upset will ordinarily feel she is blaming him. A woman does not usually understand how much her discontent stresses her man.

Women often feel that their husbands do not hear them or take their problems seriously. Yet in many cases, it is just the opposite. Men take women's complaints too seriously, resulting in unnecessary stress and withdrawal.

A couple we talked with had just moved to our city, where he had a job, and she had not yet made any new friends. She was unhappy and told him that she did not like it here, did not want to stay, and that if he did not find another job in the next year she was leaving. It got his attention. Two weeks later she had her house organized, had made several friends, was playing tennis and had been invited to go horseback riding. She told him things were better and she now liked it here. Yet he talked to a job recruiter, which surprised her. He had it locked in his mind that she was not happy, and he told her there was no way she could convince him she was happy when she had been so miserable two weeks earlier. It took us most of a session to convince him to take her at her word.

Most men seem to be programmed to take complaints from women at face value, while women are programmed to express their troubles casually without giving it a great deal of importance. Men tend to read more significance into a complaint than the women mean to convey. A man whose wife is often upset may conclude that she is permanently miserable and cannot be "fixed." Yet he will still feel responsible for her and inadequate because he cannot make her happy. He may strive to be an unassailable breadwinner, always at work, or he may withdraw into the television.

Remember that women are much freer in voicing complaints. You should not take each complaint so seriously. Allow the times she looks happy or says she is happy to count as much as when something goes wrong.

Remember that your mate probably takes your complaints more seriously than you realize. Be careful how strongly you express your unhappiness. And if you are happy with him, be sure it shows. Ask him if he thinks you are generally pleased with your life with him. If you are usually happy but occasionally upset and he thinks you are upset all the time, why the incorrect impression? Stop shooting and try troubleshooting.

Origins of fixers

Why are men fixers? Evolution provides an explanation. Throughout the ages, women with small children were extremely vulnerable and required the support of the men. Men who sought to fix things would mate more often, support their wives better, and have more surviving offspring. So men are naturally programmed to try to fix whatever is troubling women, and to interpret complaints as pressure to work harder and provide better. Women are freer to complain, to let men know how they feel and what they need.

Imagine for a moment that it were otherwise. A man and a woman are huddled in a primitive shelter, eighty thousand years ago, somewhere in middle Europe. Snow is falling outside, the cold wind is blowing through the cracks in the makeshift hut, firewood is gone and so is the food. The two converse:

> SHE: Org, it is so cold in here. I'm freezing, and I'm hungry. The wind is coming through the cracks in our hut, the fire is about to go out, and we have no meat left. I'm afraid the children will starve and die.

> HE: Enga, I know just how you feel. I too share the same feelings. I too feel cold, and I am hungry, as you are. I also worry about our children, just as you do. We had some really terrible winters a few years ago, when I was a teenager. I almost froze to death myself. So I really do understand.

What is wrong with this picture? What is wrong with this *man*? Any normal man would feel tremendously inadequate about not providing better. He would experience intense pressure to gather more firewood, fix the cracks in the shelter, hunt a rabbit, or do *something* to try to solve what is troubling his wife.

Perhaps ten thousand years ago a man roamed the Earth who was completely comfortable when his wife was upset. Tragically, his wife and children did not survive the long, cold winter, and his laissez-faire inclinations perished with them. Men who are fixers pass their genes to the next generation, continuing the strong male inclination to try to fix it when a woman is upset.

It is easy for a woman to condemn a man for wanting to fix things instead of working to understand her feelings. You might make allowances. The "fix it" response has been essential for human survival for hundreds of thousands of years and is by now strongly inbred into the normal male character. Is it fair to condemn a man for trying to be helpful, even when the way he does it is not just what you wanted?

While it generates its fair share of troubles, the natural programming does prevent a few follies that could easily occur without it. We have a couple of acquaintances who, by natural temperament or by sheer acts of will, have managed to overcome any tendency to be stressed when a woman is upset with them. Both were good at listening and understanding, and both were also philanderers. One confided in me the secret of his success. "There is not a woman anywhere who cannot be seduced by a man who is willing to stay up until 3 A.M. listening to her problems." From hearsay, we suspect he well knew. The other fellow, who was married, talked to women at great length about their problems, including their problems with him. When a woman felt insecure, or perhaps used when he went home to his wife, he fully understood her feelings and was warm and supportive. He was so sympathetic that it was hard for any woman to stay mad at him. A lady would tumble into bed for another round, followed by another round of being upset at him, which he also understood. We had the opportunity to talk to one of his paramours. She found it impossible to break up with him, since he was giving her the understanding she always wanted, but also impossible to continue, since she could never figure out where she stood with him.

Perhaps this may help women readers.

♀ Are you annoyed with your mate because he has to "fix" everything and cannot simply listen to you when you are upset? Realize it could be worse. You could have a man who simply listens to you, on and on, and never fixes anything.

Origins of expressers

There is a complementary relationship between women expressing feelings and men responding to them. Nature programs women to express feelings, alerting others to their concerns, and it programs men to hear their concerns. If nature had not programmed someone to try to address your concerns, then what would be the advantage of expressing your feelings in the first place? If nobody were concerned when you are upset, what would be the point of ever talking about what is upsetting you? Sure, it can feel good to express feelings, but nature does not usually incline us toward activities that waste our time, just to make us feel good. Clearly, something more is involved.

It is more than happenstance that women express their feelings more openly and forcefully than men do. Whether upset, angry, worried, cold, hungry, frightened, or just lonely and neglected, women profit by saying it and being heard. A woman who expresses her feelings invites her husband and her broader community to take her predicament seriously, and perhaps gain invaluable assistance. Expressing feelings confers a real survival advantage and is by now built into the human temperament.

In expressing their feelings, women also monitor the pulse of the community and express its concerns. Gossip, whether warmly sympathetic or harshly judgmental, is a way of sharing information about community members and holding them publicly accountable. Why do women gossip much more so than men?[3] Remember that through hundreds of thousands of years, it was essential to yoke the wills of men to the support of the women and children. So while women bore children and tended them, and men supported the women and children, each woman had an additional job as well: It was her job to assure that her man was doing his job. Through gossip, women praise those who contribute and censure the egotists, bums, miscreants and outlaws.

In small, tightly-knit communities, gossip is a powerful mechanism of rewards and punishments. An upset individual who expresses her own anger upsets those who listen and sympathize, and invites her friends to share her grievances and uphold her cause. The man who mistreats his wife or merely neglects her might be in for some harsh judgment, and quickly. She shares her pain with her kin and close friends, who talk to their kin and close friends, and so on, throughout the community. By evening, a friend or family member takes the fellow aside, informs him that he is causing trouble for himself and for everyone else, and suggests that he shape up. In a modern society, when we live far from our families and may not even know our neighbors, gossip has lost some of its bite. But it still remains a potent force of social control.

Men provide, women judge

We can say that society trains males to be more openly competitive, and surely it does. But why? Men compete in various ways, according to what is important to a culture. Competition can be as overt as a foot race or as subtle as men competing by trying to appear more co-operative and less competitive than anyone else. And competition appears to be a human universal.[4] Among the primitive Ache of South America, hunters share the meat in a communal pool so that all families benefit equally, regardless of who hunted well and who failed. The arrangement appears to eliminate advantages and create social equality, but there is more to it. The best hunters are more apt to have lovers and have more children than the inept hunters. So while the men share equally, the women still go for those who produce.[5] Winning confers a genetic advantage. Male competition is also obvious in lower primates. Male chimps work hard for status, and strife between male rivals is frequent, while females settle into more stable coalitions.[6] The evolutionary explanation, recall, is that higher status usually provides additional mating opportunities, which benefit male genes far more than female genes.

Among men, competition is not simply for power over other men, although it is that as well. It is for achievement and recognition in whatever the culture prizes. Men strive to show themselves well-informed, courageous, adequate to the task at hand, and willing to do whatever is required. The implicit message is, "Consider me, I under-stand what is going on. I am the man with the plan and I have the courage and muscle to carry it out. I can be a leader here, or at least a major contributor." Each is striving for standing as a team player and an asset to the group pursuit. To a woman, a man is saying, "I am somebody. I have standing. Count on me. I can provide whatever you need and take care of you." In short, he is saying, "I can fix it."

Just as it is his job to support the family, it is her job to judge his contribution to see that he is doing what she requires. Women admire men who contribute, and women also condemn and scorn those who fail to support them or who treat them badly. In the face of hardships and shortages, the tendency to be upset and to judge and accuse provides a distinct advantage. The woman who condemns a man for his failings pressures him to work harder and provide more for her. Yes, women are more easily offended than men and are more judgmental. See it not as a weakness, but as the adaptive asset that it is.

Women see men as powerful and privileged, in spite of their obvious weaknesses, which can be explained. Viewing men as powerful frees women to push their own demands, thereby benefiting themselves and their children. Nature selects for the woman who feels a man could and should be doing more for her, if only he would. Conversely, nature selects against the woman who is aware that her anger stresses her man and wears him out. Men go along with the ruse, because revealing weakness disqualifies them as providers and limits their progeny. Men and women accept the pretense because each benefits genetically from seeing men as stronger and women as subordinate.

Manhood must be achieved

Margaret Mead makes an observation about primitive societies that seems to apply to modern society as well: "The small girl learns that she is a female and that if she simply waits, she will some day be a mother. The small boy learns that he is a male and that if he is successful in manly deeds some day he will be a man, and will be able to show how manly he is."[7]

Manhood must be achieved. Young boys feel they must prove themselves real men, and strive to do so, while young girls grow naturally into women. In groups, boys require strength and confidence in one another, and haze those who appear weak or afraid. Girls expect openness and sharing, and are more apt to accept fears and weaknesses.

Why the difference? See manhood as the strength, courage, honor and success required to win a woman and then to support her. Traditionally, a young man must prove himself to gain a wife, whereas a young woman is marriageable simply because she is young and healthy and therefore presumably fertile. Young men gain by striving for manhood, and the inclination is passed along, whereas young women would not gain as much by similar strivings.

An analysis of 93 cultures shows that boys, more than girls, are generally taught to show more fortitude and are expected to face hardships without complaining.[8] So male toughness is not simply a Western custom, but is common across cultures.

Incidentally, the same analysis shows that girls are more industrious, more responsible and more compliant with authority than are boys, which is to say that girls are generally more consistent and more productive than are boys. These qualities surely contribute to school performance through high school, where two out of three honor students are girls and two out of three dropouts are boys. Indeed, in every level of education the boys are falling behind,[9] and it is not clear what might be done about it.

Mothers and fathers

A similar pattern is seen in how we interact with our children. Mothers are usually freer in expressing their feelings, while fathers want to fix whatever is wrong. When the youngster crashes his bike and skins himself up, mom nurtures and comforts him, while dad helps him fix the bike and gets him back on it. Neither approach is better, and it would be fair to say that the two parents each provide something important and complement each other.

Fathers are often the enforcers, as noted earlier, and mothers who are upset with their children often pull the fathers into the battles as well. Suppose dad is not particularly concerned about the curfew, and the teenager is out an hour later than he agreed upon. If mom is not concerned about it herself, or manages it calmly, dad stays out of it. If mom is really worried and upset and complains that the youngster does not care about how much he worries her, then dad will probably see it as a serious offense as well. If it is upsetting his wife, it is also thereby upsetting him. Many men support their wife with the children, whether or not they would otherwise be concerned about a problem.

As an old saying has it, "When mama ain't happy, ain't nobody happy!" Men take their emotional cues from their wives, and over-respond when under pressure.

SHE *(worried and upset about her son):* Where is he? He never tells me where he is going, and he never gets in when he says he will. I'll be up all night worrying.

HE *(to himself):* Damn him! Wait until I get my hands on that boy.

As is typical of fathers, he is stressed by his youngster upsetting his wife. He will jump on the son, maybe too hard, and his wife may be upset with him for overreacting. One of the traditional understandings between father and son is, "Whatever, just don't upset your mother."[10] When the youngster does upset his mother, the father jumps in to correct him.

Men want to be needed

To not be needed by your wife is to suffer a slow death, suggests John Gray. Men find meaning in providing for a wife and family and in being appreciated for it. Being needed helps bond a man to his family, whereas men who are unnecessary are freer to go.

Our current feminist ideology suggests that women should be able to do everything on their own so that they do not need men and can make it just fine on their own if necessary. Furthermore, women should appear independent or strive for independence, even when they do need men, so that they do not appear weak or needy.

The striving for independence is admirable, but it can be taken too far. We do need each other. Strong bonds to family and friends make our lives more meaningful, and most of what we accomplish in this world is a result of working together. And men and women do surely need each other not just for companionship but to establish the families which give us a sense of real belonging.

Unfortunately, the idealization of independence adds one additional obstacle to forming solid families. Strength and independence are fine qualities, but we should always be aware of the many ways we do need each other.

Appreciate and acknowledge to each other the important ways that being together strengthens you and makes your life more meaningful.

Procrastination

Like anything else, the expresser–fixer exchange can also go terribly wrong. The marital version of procrastination involves a request, the expectation that the request be honored, the appearance of an agreement to comply, but then delay, the frustration and anger over the delay, further requests, and further delays.

Ms. asks her Mr. to take out the garbage. He is watching TV or otherwise occupied, so he says he'll get to it in a minute. He does not really feel like taking out the garbage, and he puts it off and forgets about it for the time. So she reminds him again, and he agrees again, and on and on it goes. Along the way, she has the garbage on her mind as she tracks whether it stays or goes. She feels thwarted, frustrated, and angry, and does not want to nag but feels forced into it. He wants to be left alone, but feels nagged and resents it.

The procrastinator is an illusionist, obviously, in that he creates the impression that he will do something that he will not do or will not do without further harassment. Is it any wonder that his counterpart feels fooled, and furious?

Leave aside the issue of why men usually have the job of taking out the garbage. Chores must be assigned in some manner, and our culture seems to consider carrying garbage a manly chore and a courtesy to the wife.

Perhaps the procrastinator who agrees to take out the garbage means to do so, sort of, but he means to do so when he feels like it. It may be a long while before he gets to it, and in the meantime he may forget, and when he does remember he may not feel like it. And while she has figured out the pattern from prior experience, she can either accept him at his word or start nagging immediately. So she accepts his pledge, but then feels fooled when he forgets and the garbage remains untended. And then eventually, she nags.

On the other hand, perhaps the wife seems too formidable to argue against and the fellow therefore feels that he has no choice but to agree or at least pretend to agree to take out the garbage even though he would rather not and has no plan to do so. A forced concession is not the same as an agreement freely made.

So far as the fellow feels it is fair and freely accepts the chore, then a time management principle is in order. You can either take out the garbage when asked, or you can tie a string to your finger or write yourself a note and tape it up where you will see it, and then take out the garbage when you notice that reminder. But note here that creating a reminder which you will later note and then doing the chore means you are really doing two chores instead of just one. A simple chore has become a reminder and a chore.

We suggest that couples begin with a look at how chores are assigned and what is fair and whether the fellow feels that he really should take out the garbage. So far as he accepts the chore, then it is all so much simpler and more civil when he does it as requested and without delay or further reminder.

So far as he resents taking out the garbage, some negotiations are in order. He should present his opinion on what he feels is fair, and she should listen. And then the two must hash it out and come to an agreement.

A friend of ours gets up and cheerfully completes a reasonable request. He tells us he is so prompt that his wife sometimes reminds him that she never meant he has to do it immediately. But he has it figured. Why do a reminder and then a chore, when you can do the chore, have it out of the way and off your mind, and forget the reminder altogether. We might add that he does not agree to every project his wife requests. He figures out what he feels is fair and chooses how to spend his time. He tells his wife when a request does not fit in his schedule, and they hash it out.

 Be prompt when you accept a request, and candid when you do not. Procrastination involves you in the worst of all possible worlds.

"I meant what I said and I said what I meant," says the trustworthy elephant again and again in *Horton Hatches the Egg.* In the matter of chores, it is both honorable and well worth the trouble to state our real position and then follow up in our actions. It is particularly not a good time to keep your opinions to yourself. And while the "hundred percent trustworthy" standard may be a shave too high, it would not hurt us to mean more of what we say and to say a bit more of what we mean.

Job Conflict Triggers Marital Conflict

With so many women working outside the home, facing the usual tensions and conflicts there, work concerns are brought home and into the evening conversation. It would seem to be a natural opportunity for men and women to share their troubles, understand and support each other, look at their alternatives, and bond together against an unfriendly world. But when women talk with their husbands about their job frustrations, something goes wrong. Instead of sharing counsel as friends and allies, mates become antagonists and conversations head south. Work troubles brought home quickly turn into marital troubles. Neither men nor women understand how and why these conversations fail, or what to do about it.

She complains, he stews

After a stressful day, a woman wants to talk about it, share experiences, express her fears and frustrations, and be listened to and understood. As usual, the man is inclined to solve whatever is wrong, and quickly. Here is the typical pattern, which occurs and reoccurs in marriage after marriage:

Suppose the woman complains about her boss. "He drives me crazy. I swear, the man cannot make a decision. I have to figure out what to do, and take some responsibility before the roof falls in. And then when he gets nervous or something goes wrong, he wants to know why I did what I did. All he cares about is covering his own buttocks."

Her husband tries to resolve the problem, but more quickly than is realistically possible. Initially, he instructs her on how to fix the work situation. "Just refuse to do anything to help him, and then see what happens!" Or he provides some other equally simple solutions for what are almost always complex organizational problems. "You ought to get everyone together and tell him what an awful job he is doing."

When she will not take his advice and solve the problem, he wants her out of there. "Well, if you are so unhappy there, you ought to quit."

You would think the conversation should be more complicated than this. But honestly, we are not oversimplifying it. We cannot tell you how many husbands we have seen give some variation of these two responses, and nothing more. No attempt to support her feelings, understand the situation, or map out the realistic options and the consequences of each one. Nothing. The typical husband tells his wife to confront her boss, or whoever is causing her trouble, and get the problem resolved. When she will not do so, he tells her to quit.

Understanding and support

Job situations are typically complicated, and quick solutions are seldom helpful. You rarely get anywhere telling off your boss. You cannot risk leaving the job undone so that your superior looks bad, and it is not easy to organize your fellow workers to band together and confront the boss. Is quitting a realistic option? A woman who is serious about her job and career is not going to quit over some ordinary job friction any more than a man would.

A man needs to recognize that what his mate wants is mainly understanding and sympathy. She wants to unwind, to share with her mate, to be appreciated for the tough job she is doing. It is not strictly true that she does not want to hear solutions, but the order is important. She would be willing to hear solutions later, *after* he first shows that he understands her feelings and appreciates her grasp of the situation.

♂ Remember to understand and appreciate first, and only then look at solutions. Recognize that many irritating work situations are not easily resolved, and we do well to accept it and make the best of it.

♀ Realize how much stress your husband probably experiences from your own hard day at work. Men are poorly equipped to hear how their wives are mistreated while they are helpless to do anything about it.

Failed chivalry

However antiquated it seems today, a man still wants to protect his woman from the hazards of the outside world. To do so is honorable, to fail to do so is unmanly and beneath contempt. In another time it would be called chivalry. The knight would pledge to defend the lady, so that any attack on her honor was an attack upon his honor as well. How does a man feel when his wife tells him how badly she was beat up at work? He must recognize that she has been out fighting the foe while he was helpless to protect her.

Much of the conflict for working women is with their supervisors who have power over them, and many of those supervisors are men. And therein lies an additional stressor. To a man, it is unnatural to have his woman away from home and subject to the power of another man. Were the conflict among women, he might figure that it will work itself out. But when another man is mistreating her, it calls forth a primal male instinct to protect what is his. A man who cannot or does not protect his woman from other men must wonder whether she is still his woman. Obviously, nature selects against the man who would be comfortable allowing another man to have his way with her.

A man feels he must either support his wife within the group so that she is respected, or rescue her and take her away from those who mistreat her. And thus the usual male responses: He commands his wife to tell off her boss, and thus gain respect, or to quit the job and get out from under his control.

So long as a woman wants to keep her job, she cannot do either. To get along at work, she must consider what her boss wants over what her husband wants her to do. And that is the stressor. It comes across to a man not as a simple practicality but as a major infidelity. She appears to be loyal to her boss, complaining but doing as he commands, and refusing her husband. As the husband sees it, the boss has power over his woman, whom he is powerless to protect, and she is willfully going along with it. It goes over badly. He is shamed and angry, although only the anger shows. He is mad at her refusal to change the situation. She feels he is attacking her instead of trying to help her figure out her problem.

Sympathy

Perhaps women can see something understandable here, in what would otherwise appear to be a gross lack of sensitivity. Men who were unconcerned when hostile outsiders took control of the women would have hardly passed along their genes. Men are hardwired to react strongly when belligerent outsiders attempt to control or mistreat their women.

Perhaps men can better understand their own stress and frustration when faced with an upset wife who must submit to an insensitive boss. New times call for new responses. Heroism does not always mean protecting your woman from other men who seek to take advantage of her. The real heroism today can be protecting her, and yourself as well, from the nightmare of taking it all too seriously. The real enemy is not the boss but the sense of shame that separates and isolates you from your mate.

 Recognize your impulse to protect at all costs, and then avoid acting on it. Your real battle is in your own heart. Stay available.

CR SO

Part IV.
Backwards into the Future

May you live in interesting times!

— ancient Chinese curse

Sweeping changes are underway in gender relations, as material prosperity and reproductive choice allow women the freedom to limit their families and pursue career options. Our expectations of love and marriage are also changing. We look for personal fulfillment, more so than did earlier generations who sought to fulfill their responsibilities and struggled simply to survive. We want more permissive relationships which allow us to be and do whatever we want, free from traditional gender patterns. We feel we have the right to expect the best, and our wondrous expectations blind us to the practicalities of managing ordinary relationships. We no longer make as many allowances for human nature as our grandparents once did.

Human nature continues to guide our choices. Unfortunately, various facets of human nature exist not because they are adaptive to our futures or even to our present lives, but merely because they were adaptive for our ancestors. Thus, we rely on whatever onboard mechanisms that have survived in eras long past to carry us into a new and unforeseen future.

It is a haphazard undertaking, with no guarantees. In the midst of so many changes, some aspects of gender relations seem to remain relatively stable regardless of social customs. To the extent that these reflect something inherent in human nature, we do well to take them seriously.

CR SO

10.

The Rise and Fall of Fatherhood

A man in the home is worth two in the street.

— Mae West

We have competing opinions of fathers. On the one hand, our modern society presents us with a barrage of accusations about men in general and fathers in particular, and natural sympathies go with the accusers. On the other hand, careful observation shows that involved fathers benefit their wives and children in a broad variety of ways, financially of course but also socially and emotionally. How do we make sense of fathers?

Two Parents

We mentioned that relatively lasting pair bonds came into vogue among our early ancestors about 1.7 million years ago,[1] and have remained the standard and most typical arrangement since then. So in spite of the sneaking and cheating, the briefer life spans, and an ample number of impermanent arrangements, most of our ancestors who passed along their genes were what we today term "married."

Out on the Savanna some five million years ago, our hominid ancestors were up walking on two feet with their hands free to carry the camping gear and the groceries. About a million years after that, hominid brains began to grow in size, from the one pound mini-calculator similar to that of a chimpanzee to the sophisticated three pound wonder brain that is standard equipment in the modern human head. The larger brain takes longer to mature, so human infants became increasingly helpless at birth and took considerably longer to become even modestly self-sufficient. Most primate infants can cling to their moms at birth or soon after, making them easy to carry, and can scamper on their own, but not human infants, who must be held. So travel among our early ancestors came to require two functional individuals working together, one to carry the infant and one to carry the gear. Who better to provide the assistance than a committed mate? It was about this time that human groups organized into families headed by bonded parents. How convenient!

A larger brain is a high energy luxury. The three pound human brain accounts for about 2% of our normal body weight but consumes fully 20% of our metabolic energy. So a larger brained ancestor must find ways to attain the additional nutrition, or else it starves and dies out. The introduction of fathers supporting mothers and offspring surely provided a share of the additional resources necessary for higher intelligence.

While a father and mother working together should provide about twice the resources as a mother going it alone, the cumulative results were considerably more than that. If a mother could subsist on her own, the extra resources a second parent provides are available for comfort, security, and most importantly, for innovation. The inclusion of the father into the family provided a winning edge, yoking the man to the support of his wife and her children, and later to agriculture and its abundant food production, and to increased specialization, trade, and civilization , and eventually to the material abundance of the industrial revolution. Fatherhood has been a sterling win for men, women, child-ren, material comfort, social stability and cultural advance. Fatherhood seems to be the goose that laid the golden egg.

Fatherhood among animals

Most birds but only a few mammals bond together to raise their young.

Among Snowy Owls, the mom who sits the eggs has a full time job, due to the frigid temperatures, and must rely on her mate, who hunts lemmings and brings them back to the nest. Dad continues to hunt as the owlets hatch and during their first weeks of life, and after that mom hunts as well as dad. Snowy owls are wonderful parents, and swallow their own hunger and allow their body weights to drop by as much as a third as they provide food for their ravenous youngsters. When sufficient prey is available, a snowy owl pair can raise a family of nine owlets in a single season under terribly inhospitable conditions and not lose a one of them.

Two parents working together to raise the young can provide a huge advance over a single parent going it alone. Is it not surprising that the arrangement has not caught on among more mammals? Among grazing animals, such as horses or deer, it is not clear how a male might contribute. Would he snatch a clump of grass in his teeth and bring it over to his missus and lay it down for her to eat it? Among predators such as bears or leopards, the male of the species could obviously help out with the provisions but instead he simply mates and goes his own way while the faithful mother stays with her youngsters and raises them. Among coyotes and various foxes and wolves, the male does bond, and he hunts and provides warm meals for his missus and the pups. Among coyotes, we might note, fatherhood has limited privileges. While the father hunts and delivers the meals, the mother establishes proprietary rights to the den and does not allow the faithful father to enter.

Why is fatherhood so common among birds but so uncommon among mammals? The answer may be in the ease with which the mother of the species can manage it on her own. A mama bird must sit the nest and warm the eggs for the chicks to survive, while a mama mammal carries her unborn youngsters inside her belly and remains mobile during gestation. And once youngsters are born, survival for chicks requires hourly food collections, while a mama mammal has an onboard supply of nutritious milk. So while male birdies who fail to bond would have few or no surviving offspring, most bachelor mammals seem to pass along their genes just fine. A similar arrangement seems to have worked well enough for our hominid ancestors, up until the time that children required too much for a single mom to handle on her own.

Bonded primates

Among primate species, most males mate casually while others commit and stay. Primate males who stay and bond may be heading down the long trail to becoming "dads."[2]

Gibbons, also known as small apes or lesser apes, are best known for their breathtaking acrobatics a hundred feet high or more up in the trees. An adult gibbon can swing from branch to branch at a speedy 35 miles per hour, and can soar as far as 50 feet in the air as he swings from one tree to another. Gibbons can do almost everything but actually fly.

Gibbons mate for life, and a family consists of a bonded adult pair and their juvenile offspring. The families use hooting calls and menacing gestures to announce their presence and to warn trespassers away from their precious fruit trees, with the adult pair standing together and youngsters sometimes joining in. The females carry the infants and feed and tend to them, while the males seem to have no further family responsibilities past protecting their territory. The males gain from the continuing mating opportunities, and the bonded pair provides improved protection for the youngsters.

Pair bonding occurs infrequently among primates, in about six percent of primate species, and the bonded males guard the families but are not seen to contribute the material support that we would ordinarily associate with fatherhood. Among primates, the bonded pair appears to be a halfway step between stag arrangements of unbonded males and the active and supportive participation we expect of our own human fathers.

Ancestral fathers

As our mating ancestors bonded together, the males of the species became progressively more involved in supporting the females and in raising the youngsters. Bonding with a female provided a continuing sexual relationship, established a social alliance, and protected the children against outsider males who might find the female appealing but would consider her children unwelcome nuisances. Those bonded males who more actively supported the mother and her children became our first fathers, providing more for the youngsters and also gaining the additional respect from the mothers, which would surely translate into additional romantic invitations and thus additional progeny. By choosing contributors over slackers, our mothers themselves lured men into families and helped cultivate fatherhood as an integral feature of the early human community.

While pair bonding began some 1.7 million years ago, it is reasonable to expect that fatherhood evolved gradually among bonded pairs, with the males gradually relinquishing their independence and contributing more to support their families and raise their youngsters. Males thus progressed from independents to bonded partners, and then from there into integral members who contribute significantly to the families.

Evolution does not change human nature quickly because we foresee a future need, but gradually as a course of small changes provides small gains for each succeeding generation. Our hominid males became bonded partners and then fathers, not all at once because they could foresee it contributing to the wonders of civilization but gradually, one step at a time, as each step along the path provided a small survival advantage. Only in hindsight do we see the fatherhood arrangement as an essential requirement in our long journey from just another hairy primate to the most intelligent and highly accomplished species on the planet.[3, 4]

New expectations

Joint parenting arrangements mean that we must each expect more out of a prospective mate. Rather than settle for any strong male with good genes, females would seek males who would provide resources and remain committed. Rather than settle with any fertile female, the males would look for faithful mates to ensure that the rug rats they toiled to raise were their own rug rats.

An odd asymmetry exists here. A marriage can be between a man and a woman and maybe a second woman as well, as happened in various earlier societies. The man is still obligated to support his wives, however many he acquires, along with their various children, and fidelity is still required of a woman to ensure that her children are also his children. While multiple wives have been widely tolerated in earlier cultures, it his highly unusual for two men to join together to share a wife. Men are severely agitated by uncertain paternity. Two or more women may be willing to share a particularly good provider, as each can calculate whether she is getting a sufficient share, while a man is unwilling to share access to a single woman, where his genes may loose out altogether.

Our ancestors continued as hunter-gatherers until the arrival of agriculture, about ten thousand years ago. Unlike hunting, which was sport, or gathering, which could be pleasant, clearing the land and manhandling an ox and plow across miles of furrows was endless hours of strenuous toil.[5] Agriculture, of course, provided the abundance of food that supported larger populations and freed men to specialize and join together in productive ventures that would grow into what we now call civilization.

Fortunately, the rudimentary social arrangements were already in place. Men gradually signed on to the harder workloads, as a way to support a woman and a family, while women accepted the fidelity requirement, in exchange for the improved material prosperity. Early agricultural societies were strongly patriarchal and placed on women some of the strictest requirements for fidelity.

Patriarchy

A quirky finding made a splash with the media several years ago and has been spoofed as "Whatever you say, Dear." In his study of over a hundred newlyweds, researcher John Gottman observes that men who willingly comply with what the wife wants will have considerably better marriages than men who object and resist.[6] And when these happily married couples do disagree, the men actively search for common ground and compromise. "I wouldn't think of making a decision she disagreed with," comments one of the compliant men in the Gottman study. "That would be very disrespectful."

Obviously, compliance with expectations is important in any good relationship. It is the asymmetry here that makes the finding so noteworthy. It is the willingness of the fellow to comply with what the wife wants that is the crucial component, and not the converse. Whether the wife will comply or not comply with her husband seems to be considerably less important.

While various explanations can be offered, the findings fit easily into our traditional concerns. Women have had to rely on men to support and provide for them, over the ages, so it has been essential for a woman to see that a man who shares her sexual favors can be counted upon to do what she requires. Basically, these splashy findings fit with everything else we have been seeing.

A housewife with three small children offered her opinion: "Women want to be sure," she observed. "We have to know that a man is going to be loyal and keep his promise to take care of us. We have to know he is going to do things our way."

Additional benefits follow. Wives whose husbands respect their wishes are apt to be gentler when broaching a difficult topic, while those whose husbands resist are apt to start out caustic and continue. A gentler introduction to a problem vastly improves the chances of a civil conversation and a successful resolution.

Does all this mean that men should try harder to understand their wives and to meet their expectations? The quick and easy answer is yes, sure, of course. These findings do strongly suggest that a man who wants a satisfactory marriage must learn to cooperate and compromise.

Learn to listen to your wife, understand her concerns, cooperate with her on the small stuff and, when interests do collide, seek a mutually tolerable compromise instead of going off on your own.

Yet relationships are complex, and we should expect better results when men and women work together and compromise.

Nominal heads

Traditionally, men have been considered the heads of households, in what might today be considered a sexist arrangement. But step behind the appearances and consider the power differences. In arguments, when interests conflict, women usually dominate while men concede, placate, or withdraw. When men appear to head the household, it may be because women support them and want them to appear that way.

Look at why. Traditionally, the man was expected to commit himself to the support of his wife and children. In return, so far as he upheld his responsibilities, he was honored as the head of the family. See the trade-off? In exchange for supporting his wife, doing what she and the children require of him, deferring to her when she is upset with him, and losing when he tries to argue against her, he was honored as the head of the family.

Such arrangements have something for each. He gets the honor, and she benefits from his support. So the supposedly patriarchal arrangement benefits women every bit as much as men.

In marriages in which the woman openly heads the family, where is the trade-off? She is officially in charge, and she wields much of the covert emotional power as well, leaving him with little respect and little voice. What is in it for him? Or for her, since she has no reason to respect him?

Patriarchy today is itself a masquerade, a convenient fiction in which the actors stay in character and the audience agrees to accept the production as just what it pretends to be. See patriarchy as an artfully crafted but fragile arrangement, honoring men who stay and support their families in order to encourage them to do so. The advantage is intact marriages, holding men and women together for their mutual benefit and for the benefit of the children.

The traditional Christian support for men as heads of households has surely helped to rebalance marriages, upholding men who stay and contribute and asking women to appreciate more and criticize less. It makes you wonder if the early Christian forefathers were wiser in these matters than our secular skepticism today would have us believe.

Women guiding men

In our age of independent women, as strange as it seems, some women we talk to expect their husbands to be the sage heads of the families, always knowing what to do, and then find themselves angry when the head of the family stumbles and does the wrong thing.

We suggest the obvious, that the woman talk about her concerns and tell her husband what she wants him to do to make things better. The objection we usually hear is that the woman wants a man who really is the head of the family and that she does not want to have to take over and tell him what to do. She fails here to realize that "head of the family" is an honorary title and does not mean "omniscient sage," or "commander-in-chief." And while she does not allow herself to tell her husband what to do, she understandably loses respect for him and gripes when he does not do as she wants.

♀ Realize that men need consultation and guidance in family matters, every bit as much as women, and find ways to respectfully suggest, coach, coax, and otherwise pull for what you feel is best. Do not confuse an honorary title with unrealistic expectations of superior command.

The research that finds egalitarian marriages are the most satisfying has an additional twist. Wife-dominated marriages are the least satisfying, and husband-dominated ones are in the middle.[7] That is, marriages in which women openly dominate their husbands tend to be more troubled and less fulfilling than those in which men appear to dominate. Men do not find them satisfying, which should be obvious, but women do not find them satisfying either.

♂♀ At the risk of restating the obvious, might we suggest again that we strive for equal participation? Is it not possible for men to be stronger and more forthright and for women to be understanding and more appreciative?

Leadership requirements

The usual imbalance in emotional power sets limits on how men and women might expect to prevail in marital conflict . If an average man is to lead, he must gain respect and must convince his wife that whatever solutions he proposes are fair and are in her best interests. Otherwise, she will continue to be upset and angry at him, and her anger will unsettle him more than his anger might unsettle her. We suspect that men ordinarily lead in families by finding compromises, as the above findings suggest, and often by settling upon something close enough to what their wives want them to do. Men who cannot find agreeable compromises lose respect, sometimes quickly, and fail as family leaders.

In contrast, a woman might prevail without earning respect and without seeking a compromise, simply by allowing her emotions to intimidate her husband and to silence him.

In the traditional Western wedding, the bride promised to "love, honor, and obey." The time when women were expected to obey is long gone—as if the average man was ever able to command his more volatile wife to obey him if she did not want to do so. But what about the honor? In the rebellion against patriarchy, that too is being lost. Honor confers respect for contributions, and men who are honored have more reason to strive to contribute than men who are scorned. "Honor your husband" can be translated loosely as, "Curtail your emotionality, listen to him and try to understand his concerns, so that he may have a real voice in the family." Otherwise, female emotions dominate and males withdraw, creating an imbalance that neither one finds satisfying.

If men were normally more forceful in marital squabbles, then an increase in female power would promote equality. But the flawed illusions of the masquerade lead to flawed policy. In so far as women are naturally more argumentive, the same solution undermines the traditional balance of marital relationships. Men withdraw in the face of female accusation, leaving marriages emotionally barren and unpleasantly matriarchal.

The grand masquerade portrays the average American family as patriarchal, with an agreement that the man is to be seen as the head of the household and the wife as subordinate. Today even that courteous pretense is quickly vanishing, as patriarchy now refers more to a form of oppression rather than a viable trade-off between men and women. So far as patriarchy implies a form of oppression, then it is good riddance to bad rubbish. So far as patriarchy is merely honor bestowed upon men who marry women and support families, we are losing yet another dimension that holds the two-parent family together.

Providers

Our typical reactions to having children reveal our traditional responsibilities. A mother with a newborn child tends to bond strongly and must tear herself away from her infant to go back to work. Meanwhile, the father cannot wait to finish whatever his wife expects of him and get back in harness and start earning the money to provide for his family.

Men ordinarily work more hours and earn more after they become fathers, while new mothers tend to work fewer hours outside the home and earn less.[8] Fathers with young children are four times as likely to work at least fifty hours a week as are working mothers with young children.[9] Fathers who work the extra hours free mothers to be involved with the children.

Furthermore, marriage itself tends to make men more productive. Married men attain faster wage growth in their first ten to twenty years of marriage, compared to men who are not married. And being married increases by almost 50% the chances that a recently hired man will attain a high performance rating. Researchers Sanders Korenman and David Neumark conclude that "marriage per se makes [male] workers more productive."[10] Men who become widowed, separated or divorced lose their productivity bonus.

Married men ordinarily bring their earnings home, meaning that the whole family benefits from their increased productivity. Marriage to a man who provides well affords mothers the choice to spend more time with their families. Men who can be expected to be good providers are considerably more marriageable. By one survey, the men who get married over the course of any year earn about 50% more than the men who do not marry.

Protectors

Men who have made the transition to fatherhood tend to be highly protective of their families. While we often associate domestic violence with marriage, the reality is quite the opposite. The combination of marriage and fatherhood offers surely the strongest protection against violence toward women and children.

Over the twenty years up to 1992, the rate of violent crimes against women was 43 per thousand for unmarried women, 45 for divorced and separated women, but only 11 for married women.[11] Married women benefited from a fourfold reduction in violence, compared to their unmarried counterparts.

And the same holds for the children. Children in reblended families are much more likely to be physically, emotionally, and sexually abused than are children living with two natural parents. While some step-parents are good as gold, most remarry for the adult companion and may not have the patience for the stepchild that trudges along in the bargain. A 2005 review finds that children living in a household with a step-parent or live-in boyfriend are nearly fifty times as likely to die of inflicted injuries as are children living with two married parents.[12]

Enforcers

Traditionally, mothers counted upon the fathers to back them up and enforce family standards. That too is changing. And when mom does not support dad, it is unlikely that dad will have the authority he would need to support mom.

When one parent is successful in promoting compliance and the other parent is ineffective, the most obvious first step is to figure out what the successful parent is doing that works and then train the other parent to do about the same things. So when a child obeys dad and ignores mom, we try to find out what dad is doing that compels compliance which mom could do to produce the same good results. It all seems so straightforward, and sometimes it is.

When dad requests something he walks over to his youngster, reaches out and makes contact, says "Hey buddy," and walks the child along with him to carry out the request. We call it "guided compliance." Implement the routine once or twice, and the child realizes that he will be forced to comply and that doing so is not so bad. So he learns to go along with it on his own. Mom has been repeating her requests when her child fails to comply, and becoming increasingly upset and yelling, all to no avail. So our first best guess is that if mom stops repeating herself and stops being upset, and does what dad does, then the child will comply for her as he complies for his dad.

Since the children are the source of so much marital conflict, permit us to offer a few key suggestions. Children do well with strict parents, and children do well with permissive parents. When parents are in open conflict over proper standards, chaos is the result and everyone loses. What reasonable child would not try to play one parent against the other, if for no other reason then just to see how far he or she can go?

♂ ♀ In front of the children, as much as is humanly possible, always support your co–parent. Afterward, alone together, you will have ample time to hash what you can agree upon and how you should parent your children. Present a united front, and hassle it out among yourselves in private.

Fashioning Fathers

We note that across species, a usual requisite of fatherhood is what biologists call "pair bonding" and what we humans call "marriage." Among animals which do not form pair bonds, such as chimpanzees and orangutans, seals and dolphins, cows and sheep, and dogs and cats, the males obviously inseminate, but it would be sloppy and too anthropomorphic to mistake mere insemination for anything resembling fatherhood. These stag males are eager to mate but show no interest at all in raising their progeny. Indeed, among lions and gorillas, a reigning male will run off the adolescent males, including his own offspring, to maintain his control over his harem. Among domesticated animals where bloodlines are important, such as thoroughbred horses or purebred dogs, the inseminating male is called a "sire" or a "stud" and goes on record as such, but he does not partake in anything resembling fatherhood Among most animals who mate in the wild, an inseminating male is termed a "mate," which refers to the act of mating and not to a continuing relation with the female and her offspring.

Not until the males bond together with females in the wild or in the human social order do we see actual fatherhood, with the males supporting their mates and the youngsters who arise from the mating.

So pairing together is the first principal feature and is ordinarily absent when the males do not participate as fathers. Among Snowy Owls, the father and mother work closely together to warm the eggs and feed the owlets. Among coyotes, foxes, and wolves, pop catches and butchers the meat with his grinders and brings it home to mom, who serves it up warm to the hungry pups. Among birds such as snowy owls and among a few mammals such as coyotes, foxes, wolves, and traditional humans, the male who bonds with the mother and helps her raise the young has made that transition into what we might rightly call fatherhood.

Conditions for fatherhood

Fatherhood in its most understandable sense has several features, although all are not present for every father:[13]

(1) A father is the biological inseminator, which is our principal standard, although men who adopt children and raise them are still very much fathers. The biological connection tends to activate what is known as "kin altruism," which is an innate tendency to love and care for our biologically related family members. Unfortunately, the kin altruism mechanism may be weak or entirely absent unless the other essential conditions are also present.

We want to see the inseminator as the father, and traditionally we required a man who inseminates to marry the mother and to take on the responsibilities of fatherhood. In the absence of a relationship with the mother or her child, we refer to a sperm provider as the "biological father," meaning that he has contributed a set of genes but is hardly a father in the broader social and moral sense. We might just as well call him the sperm producer, donor, depositor, or perhaps the "sperminator," which offer more accurate images for what this fellow typically provides.

Marriage ordinarily involves a public alliance in which a man has an exclusive right to be with the woman and, in exchange, he is committed to provide for her and for their children. Note the two asymmetries here. It commits the man to taking care of the woman and her children more so than the other way around, in that a woman normally takes care of her own children whether she is married or not. And marriage commits the woman to being exclusive with the husband, more than the other way around, in that the man must know that the children he is raising are his own children.

Generally, when men can be confident a woman and her children are their own, they form nuclear families, often close to their own folks. In societies where men are unsure of paternity, marriages are more unstable, women often live near their own folks, and a woman's brothers may be their principal male benefactors.[14] That is, the men who sire the children tend to be providers and benefactors where women are faithful, but not where women are free to sleep around. So the paternal support that helped transport our ancestors into civilization flourishes amid paternal security and not otherwise.

(2) A father has an alliance with the mother and is married to her or common-law married. Indeed, a man's initial connection to an unborn child is often through his love for the mother. Men who maintain a committed relationship with the mother are the mainstay of fatherhood and contribute willingly, while men who do not bond with the mother or who separate and divorce are often inconsistent or absentee fathers, and hardly fathers at all.

A close partnership with the mother can cover for some amount of father absence, as when work or military service takes a man away from the family for an extended time. A supportive mother convinces the children that the man is still a good father and is taking care of them in spite of his absence, and she reassures the man that he belongs and his family waits for his return.

(3) A father resides with his children and is an integral member of the family. A man who resides with the children has an ongoing opportunity to participate in raising the children and typically has responsibilities for the children whether he might wish to or not. Unfortunately, men who never reside with their children have only infrequent interactions and fail to bond properly with the children, and men who bond but are separated from their children often lose the bond.

A continuing partnership with the mother in an intact family vastly increases the chances a sperm contributor will mature into a real father and remain a real father. Unfortunately, the converse is also true. Men who provide sperm but do not partner with women and do not reside with the children seldom become participating fathers in the usual social relationship sense of the word. We want them to be fathers and expect them to be fathers, never considering that they do not experience the conditions that ordinarily transform men into fathers. As much as we might wish otherwise, the man who pumps sperm but has no relationship to the mother and is not a member of the family seldom acts as a father to her child.

Such men are broadly condemned for their irresponsibility and referred to now as "deadbeat dads," although many were only casual sperm depositors to begin with and hardly fathers in any social sense at all. Sperminators are still called "fathers," as a way to assign responsibility, but are no longer integrated into the family and so remain very much outsiders. The government can force these men pay for the insemination, but it has no means to turn casual inseminators into authentic fathers. All this suggests that there are limits to how far we can stretch the social fabric of fatherhood and still expect men to take on the responsibilities.

Only a century ago, the extended family was the norm. And in our earlier years, children were often raised communally, with assorted grandparents, uncles and aunts, and older siblings all involved, and the rest of the community stepping in when necessary. Today, with so many children raised by television and the shopping mall, the two parent family is the best we have available. Any chain is only as strong as its weakest link, so to strengthen the two-parent family we surely must support and strengthen its weakest link, which is the position of the father in the family.[15]

So long as we fail to recruit men into families, we face a lower quality of life for ourselves and we bequeath the same to our posterity.

CR   ꙮ

11.

Primal Passions
in a Changing World

Plus ça change, plus c'est la même chose.
(The more things change, the more they remain the same.)

— French proverb

Some of the sex traits we attribute here to human nature have been traditionally attributed to socialization. It has been argued that males have higher libidos because society expects males to be more sexual, or because society represses female sexuality more than male sexuality. Social considerations do guide and control our actions in many ways, some obvious and others more subtle. But when a particular trait appears regularly throughout the multitude of human cultures and throughout the whole of the animal world as well, why try to pin it on social expectation? We would not argue that tomcats pursue female cats because we expect them to, even though we do expect them to. But the argument is backwards, and unreasonable. We expect tomcats to pursue because we see them doing so, and they would do so regardless of whether or not we expect it of them. And so too with humans. We might expect young men to be more interested in casual sex than young women, but they would be that way regardless of whether you or your psychologist or a professor at Harvard expected them to be.

We expect men to be dominant when interests clash, but we observe that women are ordinarily more argumentive while men concede, placate, or withdraw. The social expectation here is worse than useless, as our expectation is exactly opposite of what we observe.

Many sex traits involve some combination of nature and culture. Chivalry is social in that we feel men ought to support women against offending men, and we apply social pressures and sanctions to compel men to act as they should. A father typically expects his children to treat their mother with respect and punishes them for crossing her. Women favor men who treat them well but condemn those who offend, as do family, friends, and society in general. Yet chivalry is also biological, in that evolution contributes to innate moral sympathies which then find expression in cultural expectations. Social animals show prototypical chivalrous conduct, allotting scarce food to females.

The exact ways men and women broker power varies across cultures and from one era to another. But given that women are more comfortable in confrontations and garner more sympathy, their concerns must carry weight. Superiority amid emotional confrontation is not a whim of our modern era, as if we could wink and make it otherwise. Women were more argumentative than men several generations ago, as the early research shows, and we might wonder if it was ever otherwise. Women are not apt to give up their natural power advantage anytime soon. And so too with chivalrous sympathies. Our outrage against men mistreating women arises out of primal sensitivities programmed in by our genes. Is there any society anywhere in which family and friends are more concerned about women using men sexually than about men using women? We have never heard of one. Indeed, it would be hard to even imagine a culture in which family and friends typically unite to protect males from sexually exploitative females instead of the other way around.

Evolution, as we have seen, accounts for a wide range of gender qualities that are not easily accounted for by strictly social explanations. It accounts for why men are drawn to strictly casual sex and why women want something more as a condition for sex. It accounts for why men are more wary of conflict and why women are quicker to take offense and express more anger. It accounts for why men feel obligated to women, bond more strongly, and are more deeply troubled when relationships fail, and for why women appear more dependent but are freer to leave relationships. It accounts for why men conceal weaknesses, and why women want men to open up and reveal weaknesses. It accounts for why women want to express their feelings while men want to fix whatever is wrong and be done with it.

Evolution provides good explanations for those gender traits which we expect and for those which we do not expect. It would take some clever finagling to try to account for all of this without considering sexual selection, and we know of no serious attempt to do so. Surely, culture shapes who we are. But it should be clear by now that our inborn natures also guide our feelings and actions, and so must shape key features of any culture.

> If we knew how important genes are,
> we would be more careful about whom we let into ours.
>
> — Bob Wyrick

Moral standards vary between cultures, between generations within a culture, and among ethnic or social classes. Yet mating has always had a substantial moral component to it, in every generation, in any society, anywhere in the world. That is because sex and progeny have been so tightly linked together, not just since the appearance of humans but all the way back to the beginnings of sexual reproduction. Consider simple lust and the rush of infatuation, the pleasure of a new love and the heartbreak of a loss, the humiliation and anger over being used, the shame of being found out, and the possessiveness and jealousy of holding on. Consider our obsessive interest about who hooks up with whom and our endless gossip, and our stern moral standards regarding who ought not to do whatever with whomever. It would be fair to say that we feel as strongly about mating as about anything else short of mortal peril. Sex continues its massive hold on our emotions because it has been a primary means by which our genes continue into the next generation or fail to do so and vanish from the earth. Should we be so surprised that is has had such a strong hand in fashioning human nature?

Maladaptive adaptations

It is an bizarre and unfortunate irony that moral sensitivities which have been highly adaptive over millions of years can turn rudely maladaptive amid changing circumstances.

Sexual conduct remains a moral quandary, with modern culture jilting between permissive acceptance of consenting relationships and strident condemnation for prohibited variations. In the midst of our liberal secular standards, an American president was impeached before a gawking public and barely escaped conviction for concealing an improper hookup with a consenting intern. Traditionally, prohibitions against sex outside of marriage stabilized families and supported alliances between families. Today, similar moral pronouncements continue but are easily ignored, and tend to undermine the credibility of our moral authorities.

Sheltering women from sex outside of marriage and forcing men to take responsibility worked wonders in traditional society, ensuring that most children had fathers. Our chivalrous sympathies supported mothers and supported fatherhood and helped carry the family genes into the next generation. In our modern era, prohibiting sex among singles seems ridiculous, and we seem unable to turn casual sex partners into fathers, and supporting single mothers seems to be the only compassionate alternative.

We have seen how chivalrous child custody arrangements that side with mothers against fathers thereby undermine marital stability and turn willing fathers into occasional visitors. As we look further, we find again and again that chivalrous support for women against men undermines fatherhood and thereby inadvertently deprives women and children of the support that fathers have traditionally provided.

In a traditional subsistence economy, the neglected woman typically wanted more provisions and more security, and a smart scolding let her man know where he stood and what she expected of him. As women today look for companionship, the same commonplace scolding that worked wonders up until modern times now promotes silence and alienation, and works against our modern yearnings for meaningful personal relationships.

And so it goes. Natural selection promotes the survival of the fittest, surely. But some take this a step too far, and assume that natural selection necessarily promotes our own survival. Evolution selects for qualities which have helped our genes survive in earlier eras. As one era gives rise to another, requirements change, and qualities which promoted survival in earlier times may or may not benefit us today.

To ensure our own survival, we would do better to rely on foresight and on bold action in service of our common interests.

Fatherhood and culture

The traditional nuclear family has been strongly challenged by a surge in the divorce rate in the 60's and 70's, and by a surge in unwed motherhood since then. Today, the mother-headed family is the most prevalent arrangement, step-families are everywhere, and the tradition of two married parents working together to raise their children is a minority arrangement.

Humankind has ridden a long way on the traditional family, with fathers providing the added resources that lifted mothers, families, and whole societies from meager subsistence toward innovation and abundance. Fatherhood has been the goose that laid the golden eggs, contributing the essential surplus that permitted one innovation after another.

By now, perhaps, we may have enough golden eggs stored up in our silos somewhere to sustain us for another decade or so. But do we really want to chance it? Do we really want to allow our culture to butcher the goose that laid all those golden eggs, and see if we might squeeze a few more individual rights and privileges out of the stupid goose? Are we willing to abandon our fundamentals while other nations catch up to us and sail on past?

In spite of its tremendous value, it should be obvious by now that fatherhood and the traditional family cannot be taken for granted. Some facets of culture turn men into real fathers, while other facets discourage fatherhood or even remove involved fathers from families. Surely one of our major social challenges is to identify those social features which promote responsible fatherhood and to muster the will to promote them so that we might reap the benefits, for ourselves and for our posterity.

America is already highly industrialized, but that should be an opportunity to advance further and not an excuse for mediocrity and stagnation. Just as fatherhood has supported our culture, so too the tilt against men and the surge of single motherhood contributes now to lower expectations and a general sense of malaise. While the patriarchal family has been under siege, nobody has proposed anything that would even remotely suffice to replace it. Patriarchy is something of a masquerade and obviously imperfect, but at the same time highly beneficial.

Would it be too presumptuous of us to suggest that we acknowledge the folly of our relationship revolution, reverse the tilt against men, support equal participation, and uphold our traditional families as a cherished heritage?

Is the masquerade required?

Many of our various masquerades have been around forever, without causing more than a manageable amount of mischief. It is only now, as women are freed from hearth and home and integrate into the public realm, that the illusions of the masquerades send us blithely along unknown paths toward outcomes we should not want to foist on our most obnoxious rivals.

We have seen here that equality between men and women is not just an agreeable ideology but that it promotes the most satisfying and most stable relationships. Over several thousands of years it would seem that men and women maintained a rough balance, with women more comfortable in confrontations and men respected for their essential contributions as providers. Chivalrous standards supported women and held men to the support of their wives and children, to the benefit of the whole community.

As women entered the public realm, the traditional sense of moral balance unraveled and society turned sharply against men. Accusations against men are now standard public fodder, under the banner of feminism or simply because we feel that way. Chivalrous sympathies continue to go with women and against men, who are increasingly intimidated and zip it around women and try to stay out of trouble.

As we recognize our natural tendencies, we can understand some of the most important trends of our times. We can see why our moral culture has tilted so strongly against men, why fatherhood has so little support, and why the nuclear family is unraveling.

We appear so fond of our masquerades, and we support them so tenaciously, that we might wonder if our shared illusions are actually requirements for living in relationships. What if we saw into our actions and wised up together, or at least enough of us wised up that it became proper to see men and women as we are instead of how nature programs us to pretend we are? Would relationships become unmanageable? Would everything unravel around us? Our own best guess is that we could still have the same advantages, but that a realistic understanding would suggest realistic ways to maintain what is right and good and try to fix what is going wrong.

Our conventional ideologies are clearly failing. Might we suggest that our schools and universities present some of the unconventional information available here and from other similar sources, not as the holy grail but as a counterbalance to the prevailing orthodoxies? It will offend the ideologues, of course. But our culture must be flexible and open to alternate ideas, if we are to formulate promising new solutions.

Perhaps the masquerades are far too ingrained to expect more than a few of us to see through them any time in the foreseeable future. So for now, those who see through the fictions are in the odd position of knowing too much and at the same time having to learn more to adjust properly in a world in which fictions are the accepted realities. Perhaps that does not seem too awful, given that the alternatives are to blindly accept the illusions or to be continually offended by them.

We doubt our material here will influence any of the diehard masqueraders. Our intent is to confirm the intuitive impressions that many of us have and to introduce practical suggestions for dealing with relationships. If your eyes are open and you have been following along, by now you probably know enough to grasp some of the realities behind our most prevalent illusions.

We hope this can serve as a survival guide for your journey among the masqueraders.

CR SO

Endnotes

These notes are based on the information available at the time. If you know of updates or corrections, please email them to the authors (rdnd at ysdu dot info). We will include them in the next printing.

Preface: The Growing Rift

1. The battle of the sexes continues according to new Gallup poll, 2008. See: http://www.prnewswire.co.uk/cgi/news/release?
2. Mike Stobbe, Record 4 in 10 babies born to unwed moms. Associated Press, November 21, 2006.
3. Linda Waite and Maggie Gallagher, *A Case for Marriage: Why Married People are Happier, Healthier, and Better Off Financially*. (NY: Broadway Books, 2000).
4. cf. Warren Farrell, *Father and Child Reunion*. (NY: Tarcher/Penguin), 2001; Bill Cosby & Alvin F. Poussaint, *Come on People:* (Thomas Nelson. 2007).

Part I. What Do Men and Women Want

1. Technically, *Homo sapiens sapiens*.

Chapter 1: The Nature of Lust

1. Ordinarily referred to as the "handicap principle."
2. Sara Hrdy, "Empathy, Polyandry, and the Myth of the Coy Female." In R. Bleier (ed.), *Feminist Approaches to Science* (New York: Pergamon, 1988).
3. R. Clark & E. Hatfield, "Gender Differences in Receptivity to Sexual Offers." *Journal of Psychology and Human Sexuality*, 2, 1989, 39–55; see D. Buss & D. Schmitt, "Sexual Strategies Theory: An Evolutionary Perspective on Human Mating." *Psychological Review*, 100, 1993, 227.
4. M. Oliver and J. Hyde, "Gender Differences in Sexuality: A Meta-Analysis." *Psychological Bulletin*, 114, 1993, 29–51.

5. H. Ehrlichman & R. Eichenstein, "Private Wishes: Gender Similarities and Differences." *Sex Roles*, 26, 1992, 399–422; J. Archer, 1996, "Sex Differences in Social Behavior: Are the Social Role and Evolutionary Explanations Compatible?" *American Psychologist*, 51, 9, 1996.

6. D. Symons and B. Ellis, "Human Male-Female Differences in Sexual Desire." In A. Rasa, C. Voge., and E. Voland (eds.), *The Sociobiology of Sexual and Reproductive Strategies* (London: Chapman & Hall, 1989), 131–146: see Archer, 1996, 913.

7. UCLA and Council on Education Study, 1997: reported by Margot Hornblower, Learning to Earn. *Time*, February 24, 1997, 34.

8. Donald Symons, *The Evolution of Human Sexuality* (New York: Oxford University Press, 1979).

9. David Buss, *The Evolution of Desire* (New York: Basic Books, 1994): cited in Beth Azar, "Modern Mating: Attraction on Survival?" *APA Monitor*, July or Aug, 1996, 30.

10. Robert Trivers, "Parental Investment and Sexual Selection." In B. G. Campbell (ed.), *Sexual Selection and the Descent of Man, 1871–1971* (Chicago: Aldine, 1972), 145.

11. George Williams, *Adaptation and Natural Selection: A Critique of Some Current Evolutionary Thought* (Princeton, NJ: Princeton University Press), 1966; Robert Trivers, "Parental Investment and Sexual Selection." In B. G. Campbell (ed.), *Sexual Selection and the Descent of Man, 1871–1971* (Chicago: Aldine, 1972).

12. Initial findings by A. Bateman, "Intra-Sexual Selection in *Drosophila*." *Heredity*, 2, 1948, 349–68.

13. In an odd anomaly in Fuji, the male damselflies are extremely rare, making them the more valuable commodity, and the females prowl for mates. It is not parental investment here which is the guiding principle but rather value created by the scarcity of the males. J. Bourne, Jr. "When damsels don't need knights" *National Geographic*, March 2007, 26.

14. See R. Wright, "Feminists, meet Mr. Darwin " *The New Republic*, Nov. 28, 1994, 36; and J. Grier and T. Burk, *Animal Behavior* (St. Louis: Mosby–Year Book, 1992), 356–357.

15. Charles Darwin separated selection into natural selection, by survival of the fittest, and a second process, sexual selection, by which mates choose and are chosen. Currently, the term natural selection is often used to refer to both survival and mate selection.

16. David Buss, "Psychological Sex Differences: Origins Through Sexual Selection." *American Psychologist*, 50, 3, 1995, 164–168.

17. John Grey, *Men are from Mars, Women Are From Venus* (New York: HarperCollins, 1992).

18. Anne Moir and David Jessel, *Brain Sex: The Real Difference Between Men and Women* (New York: Dell, 1991); John Leo, "Differences Emerge Between Male, Female." Universal Press Syndicate, Feb. 21, 1995.

19. Moir & Jessel, 1991, 48: cited in K. Peterson, "Battle of the Sexes Starts in the Brain." *USA Today*, Mar. 14, 1995.

20. Martin Seligman, *Authentic Happiness: Using the New Positive Psychology to Realize your Potential for Lasting Fulfillment*. New York: Free Press.

21. W. Gallagher, "How We Become What We Are." *Atlantic Monthly*, Sept. 1994, 38–55; John Loehlin. *Genes and Environment in Personality Development* (Newbury Park, CA: Sage, 1992); Steven Pinker provides the 50% estimate in *How the Mind Works* (NY: Norton, 1997) p 448.

22. John Archer, "Sex Differences in Social Behavior: Are the Social Role and Evolutionary Explanations Compatible?" *American Psychologist*, 51, 9, 1996, 909–917; ___ , "Darwinian and Non-Darwinian Accounts." 52, 12, 1997, 1383-84. Evolution often works in cooperation with socialization

Endnotes

23. The science of evolution involves multiple competing and overlapping principles. Traits can be selected because they benefit an individual or a genetically related kin group. Single genes can influence multiple traits, and single traits are often influenced by multiple genes. Genetically carried propensities show themselves in some circumstances but not in others.

24. Steven Pinker, *The Language Instinct*. (NY: Harper Collins, 1994).

25. R. Trivers, "Parental Investment and Sexual Selection." 1972, 153.

26. Diane Ackerman, "The Fears That Save Us." *Parade*, Jan. 26, 1997, 18–20.

27. Pope John Paul II, Truth cannot contradict truth. Pontifical Academy of Sciences, 1996.

28. The early Kinsey findings are terribly skewed by sampling biases, and he does not claim to have representative samples.

29. Bronislaw Malinowski, *The Sexual Life of Savages in North-Western Melanesia*. (New York: Harcourt, Brace, 1929), 319.

30. Technically "!Kung San," pronounced with a click.

31. M. Shostak, *Nisa: The Life and Words of a !Kung Woman* (New York: Vintage, 1981), 271.

32. Helen Fisher, *Anatomy of Love: The Natural History of Monogamy, Adultery, and Divorce.* 1992, 34–35.

33. S. Pinker, *How the Mind Works*, p. 479.

34. Symons, 1979, 138–41; C. Badcock, *Oedipus in Evolution: A New Theory of Sex* (Oxford: Basil Blackwell, 1990), 142–60; Robert Wright, *The Moral Animal*. (NY: Pantheon Books, 1994), 68.

35. R. Thornhill. "Sexual Selection in the Black-Tipped Hangingfly." *Scientific American*, 242, 6, 1980, 162–172.

36. Warren Farrell, *The Myth of Male Power* (New York: Berkley Books, 1994), 34.

Chapter 2: Emotional Firepower

1. Among our foremost experts, Howard Markman and John Gottman both emphasize surviving conflict while Gottman now also focuses on appreciation of good qualities. See Markman, "Backwards into the Future of Couples Therapy and Couples Therapy Research." *Journal of Family Psychology*, 4, 1991, 416–425; and Gottman, The Seven Principles for making marriage work (NY: Three Rivers, 1999).

2. Bernadette Gray-Little, and N. Burks, "Power and Satisfaction in Marriage." *Psychological Bulletin*, 933, 1983, 513–38; R.G. Corrales, "Power and Satisfaction in Early Marriage." In R.E. Cromwell and D.H. Olson (eds.), *Power in Families* (New York: Wiley, 1975); R. Centers, B.H. Raven, and A. Rodrigues, "Conjugal Power Structure: A Reexamination." *American Sociological Review*, 36, 1971, 264–278; R.O. Blood Jr. and D.M. Wolfe, *Husbands and Wives: The Dynamics of Married Living* (Glencoe, IL: Free Press, 1960).

3. J. Gottman and R. Levenson, "The Social Psychophysiology of Marriage." In P. Noller and M. Fitzpatric (eds.), *Perspectives on Marital Interaction* (Clevedon, Avon, England: Multilingual Matters, 1988), 182–202.

4. See: A. Christensen and C. Heavey, "Gender and Social Structure in the Demand/Withdraw Pattern of Marital Conflict." *Journal of Personality and Social Psychology*, 59, 1, 1990, 73–81.

5. See M. Komarovsky, *Blue Collar Marriage* (New York: Random House, 1962); L. Rubin, *Worlds of Pain: Life in the Working Class Family* (New York: Basic Books, 1976).

6. G. Margolin and B. Wampold, "Sequential Analysis of Conflict and Accord in Distressed and Nondistressed Marital Partners." *Journal of Consulting and Clinical Psychology*, 49, 1981, 554–67; C. Notarius and J. Johnson, "Emotional Expression in Husbands and Wives."

Endnotes

Journal of Marriage and the Family, 44, 1982, 483–489; H. Raush, L. Barry, W. Hertel, and M. Swain, *Communication, Conflict and Marriage* (San Francisco: Jossey-Bass, 1974); C. Schaap, *Communication and Adjustment in Marriage* (Lisse, the Netherlands: Swets & Zeitlinger, 1982).

7. M. Komarovsky, *Dilemmas of Masculinity* (New York: Norton, 1976); L Rubin, *Intimate Strangers: Men and Women Together* (New York: Harper & Row, 1983); H. Kelly, J. Cunningham, J. Grisham, L. Lefebvre, C. Sink and G. Yablon, "Sex Differences in Comments Made During Conflict Within Close Heterosexual Pairs." *Sex Roles*, 4, 1978, 473–479.

8. L. Terman, P. Buttenweiser, L. Ferguson, W. Johnson, and D. Wilson, *Psychological Factors in Marital Happiness* (New York: McGraw-Hill, 1938).

9. An analysis of marital case records by Agustus Napier tallies two wives dominating to each husband who dominates: *The Fragile Bond: In Search of Equal, Intimate, and Enduring Marriage* (New York: HarperCollins, 1990).

10. "Fixing Relationships," presented at the Tennessee Psychological Association convention, Nashville, Nov. 5, 1999.

11. J. Gottman, "Why Marriages Fail." *Family Therapy Networker*, May/June, 1994, 40–48.

12. Half of the cases would occur by chance, and the 85% figure accounts for 70% of the remaining cases. That leaves only 30% to be accounted for by gender-unrelated traits.

13. J. Gottman and R. Levenson, "The Social Psychophysiology of Marriage." In P. Noller and M. Fitzpatric (eds.), *Perspectives on Marital Interaction* (Clevedon, Avon, England: Multilingual Matters, 1988), 182–202; D. Baucom et al., "Gender Differences and Sex Role Identity in Marriage." In F. Fincham & T. Bradbury (eds.), *The Psychology of Marriage: Basic Issues and Applications* (New York: Guilford, 1990).

14. Robert Levenson et al., "The influence of Age and Gender on Affect, Physiology, and Their Interrelations: A Study of Long-term Marriage. *Journal of Personality and Social and Psychology*, 67, 1994.

15. John Gottman, *What Predicts Divorce*.

16. Daniel Goleman. *Emotional Intelligence*. New York (Bantam Books, 1994).

17. John Gottman, "A Theory of Marital Dissolution and Stability." *Journal of Family Psychology*, 7, 1, 1993, 57–75.

18. D. Zillman, *Hostility and Aggression* (Hillsdale, NJ: Erlbaum, 1979).

19. J. Gottman and R. Levenson, "Assessing the Role of Emotion in Marriage." *Behavioral Assessment*, 8, 1986; 31–48; Gottman and Levenson, 1988; J. Gottman, "How Marriages Change." In G. Patterson (ed.), *Family Social Interaction: Content and Methodological Issues in the Study of Aggression and Depression* (Hillsdale, NY: Erlbaum, 1990), 75–101.

20. J. Gottman, *The Marriage Clinic*. (NY: Norton, 1999), p. 7.

21. John Gottman, "Predicting the Longitudinal Course of Marriages." *Journal of Marriage and Family Therapy*, 17, 1, 1991, 4.

22. I first heard about in 1964 in a sociology text, and have seen it again in my work with relationships.

23. Susan Rogers, "Female Forms of Power and the Myth of Male Dominance: A Model of Female/Male Interaction in Peasant Society." *American Ethnologist*, 2, 1975, 727–56: see Helen Fisher, *The Anatomy of Love: A Natural History of Love, Marriage, and Why We Stray* (New York: Fawcett Columbine, 1992), 216.

24. Martin Whyte, *The Status of Women in Preindustrial Societies* (Princeton: Princeton University Press, 1978): see Fisher, 1992, 217.

25. Current thinking holds that secondary sex traits often arise from sexual selection, by male competition for females and female choice of males.

26. Donald Symons, *The Evolution of Human Sexuality* (New York: Oxford University Press, 1979): see Wright, 1994, 38 & 62.

27. Mary Batten, *Sexual Strategies: How Females Choose their Mates*. New York, Putnam, 1992.

28. Augustus Brown, "Why chickens like pretty girls ...and other bizarre animal stories. *Parade*. Nov. 26, 2006, p. 14-15.

29. Brown, see above.

30. David Givens, *Love Signals: How to Attract a Mate* (New York: Crown, 1983); Timothy Perper, *Sex Signals: The Biology of Love*. Philadelphia: ISI Press, 1985): cited in Fisher, 1992, 25 & 32.

31. Warren Farrell, *Why Men Are the Way They Are* (New York: McGraw Hill, 1986), 124–131.

32. Whyte, 1978; Fisher, 1992, 32.

33. Frans de Waal, *Chimpanzee Politics: Power and Sex Among Apes* (Baltimore: Johns Hopkins University Press, 1982, 1989), 186.

34. Robert Waterston, University of Washington. Reported in Newsweek, Sept. 12, 2005.

35. Alice Eagly, "The Science and Politics of Comparing Women and Men." *American Psychologis*, 50, 3, 1995, 145–158.

36. Buss, 1995.

37. Harriet Lerner, "The Taboos Against Female Anger." *Menninger Perspective*, Winter, 1977, 5–11.

38. Celia Halas, *Why Can't a Woman Be More Like a Man?* (New York: Macmillan, 1981): see Carol Tavris, *Anger: The Misunderstood Emotion* (New York: Simon and Schuster, 1989), 195–196.

39. Such as: Herb Goldberg, *The Hazards of Being Male* (New York: New American Library, 1976); and Jack Nichols, *Men's Liberation* (New York: Penguin, 1975).

40. Gottman, 1991, 4. The reported r=.92 correlation between the husband's heart rate and deteriorating satisfaction over the next three years accounts for 84% of the variance (which might decline on a second sample).

Part II. Chivalry Lives On

Chapter 3: Chivalrous Passions

1. Richard Lore and L. Schultz, "Control of Human Aggression." *American Psychologist*, 48, 1, 1993, 20.

2. R. Lore and K. Flannelly, "Rat Societies." *Scientific American*, 106–116, May 1977.

3. C. Southwick, "An Experimental Study of Intragroup Agonistic Behavior in Rhesus Monkeys (*Macaca mulatta*)." *Behavior*, 28, 1967, 182–209.

4. Donald Grayson, "Differential Mortality and the Donner Party Disaster." *Evolutionary Anthropology*, 1993, 151–159. We did not include here the five men who died before the encampment, from violent confrontations.

5. The one exception was a 12 year old boy, who might have been performing exhausting physical tasks along with the men.

6. Laura Ingalls Wilder, *The Long Winter* (New York: HarperCollins, 1953) 227, 252, & 308.

Endnotes

7. J.P.W. Rivers, "Women and Children Last: An Essay on Sex Discrimination in Disasters." *Disasters*, 6, 1982, 256–267; ___, "The Nutritional Biology of Famine." In G.A. Harrison (ed), *Famine* (Oxford: Oxford University Press, 1988), 56–106.

8. In the U.S., three times as many men as women are murdered each year, primarily by men. U.S. Department of Justice, Federal Bureau of Investigations, *Crime in the United States*, 1988, 11: as reported by Farrell, 1994, 214. In a *Time* tally of 464 people shot in a single week, 84% were men: "7 deadly days," *Time*, July 17, 1989, 31.

9. L. Wolf, "Human Evolution and the Sexual Behavior of Female Primates." In J. Loy and C. Peters (eds.), *Understanding Behavior* (New York: Oxford University Press), 1991, 136–137; K. Stewart and A. Harcourt, "Gorillas: Variation in Female Relationships." In B. Smuts et al., eds., *Primate Societies* (Chicago: University of Chicago Press, 1987); Frans de Waal, *Chimpanzee Politics* (Baltimore: Johns Hopkins University Press, 1982), 168; J. Goodall. *The Chimpanzees of Gombe: Patterns of Behavior* (Cambridge, Mass: Harvard University Press, 1986), 453–66; R. Wright, 1994, 51

10. de Waal, 1982; see E. Linden, "A Curious Kinship: Apes and Humans." *National Geographic*, 181, 3, 35, March, 1992.

11. B. Smuts, "Male Aggression Against Women: An Evolutionary Perspective." *Human Nature*, 3, 1992, 1–44; ___, "The Evolutionary Origins of Patriarchy." *Human Nature*, 6, 1995, 1–32.

12. de Waal, 1982; Fisher, 1992, 222.

13. Figures as of July, 1992. U.S. Department of Health and Human Services, NIOSH (Morgantown, West Virginia). Cited in Farrell, 1994, 106.

14. Les Christie, America's most dangerous jobs. CNNMoney.com, Sept. 23, 2005.

15. M. Wilson & M. Daly, "Competitiveness, Risk Taking, and Violence: The Young Male Syndrome." *Ethology and Sociobiology*, 6, 1985, 59–73: summary in Buss, 1995.

16. Indications are that hunting injuries were common among the Neanderthals, who lived throughout Europe just prior to modern man but do not appear to be our direct ancestors. Rick Gore, "Neanderthals." *National Geographic*, 189, 1, Jan. 1996, 2–35.

17. Wilson and Daly, 1985, 59–73.

18. Carrie Lukas. "In Search of Chivalry: Did it sink with the Titanic?" *National Review Online*, April 13, 2006. Available statistics vary somewhat.

19. John Barry and Evan Thomas, "At War Over Women." *Newsweek*, May 12, 1997, 38–39.

20. Laurence Vance, Fifty-four Dead Women. Blogg. Casualty figures are from 2006, when total American deaths were 2,475.

21. J. Mercy and L. Saltzman, "Fatal Violence among Spouses in the United States," 1976–85. *American Journal of Public Health*, 79, 5, 1989, 595–9. Wolfgang reports similar rates between husbands and wives from 1948–52, in *Patterns in Criminal Homicide* (New York: Wiley, 1958). These figures are for the United States and do not pertain in other nations (where women have less access to lethal weapons).

22. U.S. Department of Justice, Federal Bureau of Investigation, Bureau of Justice Statistics, *National Survey of Crime Severity* (Washington, D.C.: US-GPO, 1985): as cited in Farrell, 1994, 214.

23. R. Wright, *The Moral Animal*. (NY: Pantheon Books, 1994), 62.

24. Wright, 1994.

25. Matt Ridley, *The Origins of Virtue*. (NY: Penguin Books, 1996).

26. Marc Hauser, *Moral Minds: The Nature of Right and Wrong*. 2007

27. David Gilmore, *Manhood in the Making: Cultural Concepts of Masculinity*. (New Haven: Yale University Press, 1990).

28. Based on 1995 figures. See Guibaldi, below.

29. John Guibaldi, D.Ed., "Child Custody Policies and Divorce Rates in the US." *11th Annual Conference of the Children's Rights Council,* Oct 23-26, 1997, Washington, D.C.

30. The attained .47 correlation between joint custody and changes in divorce rates must be squared, resulting in joint custody accounting for 22% of divorce rate changes.

31. Maury Beaulier, Establishing a Presumption for Joint Physical Custody. *Transitions: Journal of Men's Perspectives.* March/April, 2006.

32. C. Buchanan, E. Maccoby & S. Dornbusch. Caught between parents: Adolescent's experience in divorced homes. *Child Development,* 62, 1991, 1008-1029; E. Hetherington & W. Clingempeel. Coping with marital transitions. *Monographs for the Society for Research in Child Development,* 57, 227, 1992, 1-242.

33. See: http://www.gocrc.com/research/jcbib.html

34. K. Alison Clarke-Stewart and Craig Hayward, "Advantages of Father Custody and Contact for the Psychological Well-Being of School-Age Children," *Journal of Applied Developmental Psychology,* 17, 2, April-June 1996, p. 239. Surprisingly, doing these everyday things together was the only predictor of psychological well-being that the study managed to identify.

35. "Are courts anti-dad?" *Parade,* July 6, 2008, p.10. Figures are from the American Coalition of Fathers and Children.

36. See the Communitarian Network: gwu.edu/ ccps/rcplatform.html

Chapter 4: The Master Illusionist

1. Sheri Prasso, "Poll: Male Bosses Favored over Females." Los Angeles Daily News, AP, March 27, 1996.

2. From Roper surveys, summarized by D. Crispell, "The Brave New World of Men." *American Demographics,* January, 1992, 38.

3. Alice Eagly, "The Science and Politics of Comparing Women and Men." *American Psychologist,* 50, 3, 1995, 145–158; A. Eagly & A. Mladinic, "Are People Prejudiced Against Women? Some Answers from Research on Attitudes, Gender Stereotypes, and Judgments of Competence." In W. Stroebe & M. Hewstone (eds.), *European review of social psychology,* Vol. 4, 1–35. (New York, Wiley, 1994); A. Eagly, H. Mladinic, & S. Otto, "Are Women Evaluated more Favorably than Men? An Analysis of Attitudes, Beliefs, and Emotions." *Psychology of Women Quarterly,* 15, 1991, 203–216.

4. R. Bellah *et all. Habits of the Heart: Individualism and Commitment in American Life* (New York, Perennial Library, 1985), 87.

5. "The battle of the sexes continues according to new Gallup poll." 2008. See http://www.prnewswire.co.uk/cgi/news/release?id=57662 ?

6. EDK Associates survey of 500 women. Redbook Magazine, November 1994, p.36.

7. Lionel Tiger, *Men in Groups,* 1969, republished in 2005.

8. Lionel Tiger, *The Decline of Males: The First Look at an Unexpected New World for Men and Women,* 1999.

9. Christina Sommers, *Who Stole Feminism?* (New York: Touchstone, 1994).

Endnotes

10. A. Hochschild, *The Second Shift: Working Parents and the Revolution at Home.* (New York: Viking, 1989, 2003).

11. J. Robinson, University of Maryland, 1985. See Marsha Mercer, "Americans May Have More Free Time Than They Realize." Scripps-Howard News Service, Aug. 7, 1991.

12. F. T. Juster and F. Stafford, "The Allocation of Time: Empirical Findings, Behavioral Models, and Problems of Measurement." *Journal of Economic Literature,* 29, June 1991, 477; see Farrell, 1994.

13. Dirk Johnson, "Until Dust Do Us Part," *Newsweek,* March 25, 2002, 41.

14. A. Hochschild, *The Second Shift,* 2003.

15. Warren Farrell, *Why Men Earn More: The Startling Truth Behind the Pay Gap—and What Women Can Do About It.* (NY: AMACOM, 2005). Farrell lists 25 factors involved in higher earnings, suggesting that women who choose these tactics can and do earn the same as men. The book is a lead title of the American Management Association.

16. Paul Basken, "Women scientists lag far behind men in patents, study says." Bloomberg, August 4, 2006

17. Murray Straus and Richard Gelles, "Societal Change and Change in Family Violence from 1975 to 1985 as Revealed by Two National Surveys." *Journal of Marriage and the Family.* 48, 1986, 465–479: see review by Christina Sommers, *Who Stole Feminism?* (New York: Touchstone, 1994), 188–208.

18. L. Bowman, Study: 1 in 11 students hurt by a date. Scripps Howard News Service, May 21, 2006. See also James Garbarino, See also, *See Jane Hit: Why Girls Are Growing More Violent and What We Can Do About It.* NY: Penguin Press, 2006.

19. In Straus and Gelles survey, 14 out of 3,500 women, or .4% of the sample, reported these most serious offenses (Straus and Gelles, 1986, 471): see also Sommers, 1994, 196–97, for figures confirming these findings.

20. The Straus and Gelles survey found that 7.3 % of the 137 women who were seriously assaulted (or .25% of all women) reported they required medical attention. M. Straus, "Physical Assaults by Wives: A Major Social Problem." In R. Gelles and D. Loseke (eds.). *Current Controversies on Family Violence.* (Newbury Park, CA: Sage, 1993). Confirmed by phone conversation with Murray Straus, Nov. 29, 1995, and Jan. 11, 1996. In a 1992 survey by the Family Violence Prevention Fund, nurses reported from 2 incidents per month in small hospitals to 8 in large hospitals, confirming generally low rates of domestic assault injuries requiring medical attention (reported in Sommers, 1994, 203).

21. The Straus and Gelles survey found that 1% of the 95 men seriously assaulted required medical attention (or .04% of the sample). Straus, 1993. Some 38% of domestic casualties in one inner city emergency room were men, vs. 62% women: "Domestic Violence Victims in the Emergency Department," *Journal of the American Medical Association,* June 22–29, 1984, 3260 (as cited in Sommers, 1994, 201). An estimate of half as many men as women requiring medical attention based on these later figures would be considered high for the general population. The 11 injuries (10 women and 1 man) located by the Straus and Gelles survey are not sufficient for a reliable comparison.

22. Based on the 16% of couples who reported assaults, vs. the .29% (.25% of women +.04% of men) who reported injuries requiring medical attention.

23. Suzanne Steinmetz, *The cycle of violence. Assertive, aggressive, and abusive family interaction* (New York: Praeger Press, 1977).

Endnotes

Part III: Tangled Together

Chapter 5: Twisted Communication

1. Tom Rusk, *The Power of Ethical Persuasion: Winning Through Understanding at Work and at Home* (New York: Viking Penguin, 1994).

2. Markman, 1991; K. Lindahl and H. Markman, "Communication and Negative Affect Regulation in the Family." In E. Blechman (ed.), *Emotions and Families* (New York: Plenum, 1990), 99–116.

3. Howard Markman, Scott Stanley, and Susan Blumberg, *Fighting for Your Marriage* (San Francisco: Jossey-Bass, 1994).

4. Janet Lever, "Sex Differences in the Games Children Play." *Social Problems*, 23, 1976, 478–487; see also Markman et al, 1994, 43–48.

5. Markman et al, 1994, 44–46.

6. John Gottman, *The Seven Principles for Making Marriage Work*. (NY: Three Rivers Press, 1999), 8-13.

7. Markman et al, 1994, 5–7.

8. Richard Driscoll, *Personal Shielding to Deflect Hostility* (Knoxville Tenn.: Westside Psychology, 2002)

9. See reviews in P. Zimbardo and M. Leippe, *The Psychology of Attitude Change and Social Influence* (Philadelphia: Temple University Press, 1991), 100–107; S. Strong, "Social Psychological Approach to Psychotherapy Research." In S. Garfield and A. Bergin (eds.), *Handbook of Psychotherapy and Behavior Change*, 2nd ed. (New York: John Wiley and Sons, 1978), 122–24.

10. John Gottman, *The Seven Principles for Making Marriage Work*. p. 22-23.

Chapter 6: Unevenly Yoked

1. See E. Pettit and B. Bloom, "Whose Decision Was It?" *Journal of Marriage and the Family*, 46, 587–595; A. Zeiss, R. Zeiss, and S. Johnson, "Sex Differences in Initiation of and Adjustment to Divorce." *Journal of Divorce*, 4, 2, 1980, 21–33.

2. In 1986, women filed 61.5% and men filed 32.6% of divorces, with the remainder filed jointly. Women without children filed a higher proportion (66%) of divorces than those without children (57%), suggesting that women do consider the children in choosing whether to leave a husband. AP, June 7th, 1989, from the National Center for Health Statistics.

3. In 1931, 49,600 divorces were granted to men (27%), and 132,600 granted to women (73%). U.S. Department of Commerce, Bureau of Census, Marriage and Divorce. 10th Annual Report. U.S. Gov. Printing Office, 1932.

4. *Time*, June 6, 1988, 35.

5. Natalie Obiko Pearson, Divorce in Japan. AP, Jan. 21, 2004.

6. C. Hill, Z. Rubin and L.A. Peplau, "Breakups Before Marriage: The End of 103 affairs." *Journal of Social Issues*, 1, 1976, 147–168.

7. E.J. Kanin, K.D. Davidson, and S.R. Scheck, "A Research Note on Male-Female Differentials in the Experience of Heterosexual Love." *Journal of Sex Research*, 1970, 6, 64–72.

8. Hill, 1976.

Endnotes

9. Figures based on corporate executives, cited in C. Casamassima, "Battle of the Bucks." *Psychology Today*, March/April, 43, 1995.

10. Citation could not be located.

11. Thomas Hargrove and G. Stempell III, "Poll: More Men than Women Eye Marriage." Scripps Howard News Service, July 29, 1993.

12. J. Smith, J. Mercy, and J. Conn, "Marital Status and the Risk of Suicide." *American Journal of Public Health*, 78, 1, 1988, 79: as cited in Farrell, 1994, 169.

13. Coined by Irina Dunn, in 1970.

14. E.W. Burgess and P. Wallin, *Engagement and Marriage* (Philadelphia: Lippincott, 1953), 270: 37.5% of men vs. 22.3 % of women report frequently conceding to avoid losing the fiancé's affection.

15. Catherine Johnson, *Lucky in Love* (New York, Penguin Books, 1992), 97–100.

16. Wright, 1994, 62.

17. 1.   .S. Begley. "Beyond stones and bones." *Newsweek*, March 19, 2007, p. 57.

18. Elaine Walster and G. William Walster, *A New Look at Love* (Reading, Mass: Addison-Wesley, 1978).

19. C.W. Hobart, "The Incidence of Romanticism During Courtship." *Social Forces*, 36, 1958, 364.

20. Kanin et al, 1970.

21. Hobart, 1958, 364; L. Peplau, Z. Rubin, and C. Hill. "Sexual Intimacy in Dating Relationships." *Journal of Social Issues*, 33, 1977, 86–109; Zick Rubin. 1973. *Liking and Loving: An Invitation to Social Psychology*. New York: Holt, Rinehart & Winston.

22. Nicholson, 1984, 57: see research summaries by: J. Bernard, *The Future of Marriage* (New Haven, CT: Yale University Press, 1982); and M. Johnstone and S. Eklund, "Life-Adjustment of the Never-Married: A Review with Implications for Counseling." *Journal of Counseling and Development*, 6, 1984, 230–236.

23. J. Veroff, E. Douvan, and R. Kulka, *Inner American: A Self-Portrait from 1957 to 1976* (New York: Basic Books, 1981) p.178. Discussed in R. Bellah et al., *Habits of the Heart*, (New York: Harper & Row, 1986), p.111.

24. 1.. Francesca Cancian, *Love in America: Gender and Self-Development.* (Cambridge, England: Cambridge University Press, 1987) 81

25. UCLA and Council on Education study, 1997. Reported by Margot Hornblower. "Learning to Earn." *Time*, February 24, 1997, 34.

26. See Casamassima, 1995, 67.

27. M. Wiederman and E. Allgeier, "Gender Differences in Mate Selection Criteria: Sociobiology or Socioeconomic Explanation?" *Ethology and Sociobiology*, 13, 1992, 115–124; M. Townsend, "Mate Selection Criteria: A Pilot Study." *Ethology and Sociobiology*, 10, 1989, 241–253. Reviewed in Buss, 1994, 46.

28. Joseph Harper, "The rhetoric of motives in divorce." *Journal of Marriage and the Family*, 55 (Nov. 1993), p.806.

29. J. Cherlin, 1978. "Women's Changing Roles at Home and on the Job." *Proceedings of a conference on the national longitudinal surveys of mature women in cooperation with the employment and training administration.* Department of Labor special report, #26; P.C. Glick, 1975. "Some Recent Changes in American Families." *Current Population Reports.* Social Studies Series P-23, #52. Washington, D.C.: U.S. Bureau of the Census: see Fisher, 1992, 193.

30. R. More and C. Winship, "Socioeconomic Change and the Decline of Marriage for Blacks and Whites." In *The Urban Underclass*, Ed. C. Jenkins and P. Peterson, (DC: The Brookings Institution, 1991), p.179.

31. See Fisher, 1992, 275–291

32. Thomas Hargrove and G. Stempell III, "Poll: More Men than Women Eye Marriage." Scripps Howard News Service, July 29, 1993.

Chapter 7: Lopsided Conversations

1. T. Fogarty, "Marital Crisis." In P. Guerin (ed.), *Family Therapy: Theory and Practice* (New York: Gardner Press, 1976); ___,"The Distancer and Pursuer." *The Family*, 7, 1979, 11–16. D. Wile, *Couples Therapy: A Non-traditional interpretation* (New York: Dryden Press, 1981); A. Christensen and C. Heavey, "Gender and Social Structure in the Demand/Withdraw Pattern of Marital Conflict." *Journal of Personality and Social Psychology*, 59,1, 1990, 73–81. Augustus Napier, "The Rejection–Intrusion Pattern: A Central Family Dynamic." *Journal of Marriage and Family Counseling*, 4, 1978, 5–12.

2. R. Schmid, "Bob's just as chatty as Cathy." AP, July 6, 2007.

3. Cited by *Washing Post* columnist William Raspberry.

4. Charles Darwin, *The Descent of Man, and Selection in Relation to Sex,* 1871: (Princeton, NJ: Princeton University Press, 1981 — facsimile edition). ___, *Expressions of the Emotions in Man and Animals* (1872 — Chicago: University of Chicago Press edition, 1965).

5. W. Goode, *Women in Divorce*. (NY: Free Press, 1969). Originally published in 1956.

6. In Monty Python, *The Meaning of Life* (MCA Home Video, 1986).

7. In a survey of 83,000 women, reported by *Ladies Home Journal*, Jan. 1983.

8. The difference between *feeling* love versus *meaning* it is from professor Peter Ossorio, at the University of Colorado, 1972.

9. Tannen, 1990, 86.

10. T. Wills, R. Weiss, and G. Patterson, "A Behavioral Analysis of the Determinants of Marital Satisfaction." *Journal of Consulting and Clinical Psychology*, 42, 1974, 802–811.

11. Tannen, 1990).

12. Cited in Steven Naifeh, *Why Can't Men Open Up?* (New York: Warner Books, 1985).

13. Reported by P. Adelmann, *Psychology Today* (May 1989), 69.

14. Study reported on National Public Radio, 1980.

15. J. Gottman, "Why Marriages Fail." 1994.

Chapter 8: Cautious Silence

1. Robert Fulghum. *All I Really Need to Know I Learned in Kindergarten* (New York: Villard, 1990), 56.

2. David Buss, "Sex Differences in Human Mate Preferences: Evolutionary Hypotheses Tested in 37 Cultures." *Behavioral and Brain Sciences*, 12, 1989, 1–49; and Buss, 1994, chapter 2.

3. Buss, 1994.

4. Farrell, 1986, especially 17–90.

5. L. Peplau and S. Gordon, "Women and Men in Love: Sex Differences in Close Relationships." In V. O'Leary, R. Unger, and B. Wallston (eds.), *Women, Gender, and Social Psychology* (Hilllsdale, NJ: Erlbaum, 1985); J. Robertson and L. Fitzgerald, "The

Endnotes

(Mis)treatment of Men: Effects of Client Gender Role and Life-Style on Diagnosis and Attribution of Pathology." *Journal of Counseling Psychology*, 37, 1990, 3–9; S. Shields, "Functionalism, Darwinism, and the Psychology of Women: A Study in Social Myth." *American Psychologist*, 30, 1987, 739–754.

6. G. Williams, *Adaptation and Natural Selection: A Critique of Some Current Evolutionary Thought* (Princeton, NJ: Princeton University Press, 1966).

7. M. Street, "What Men Will Never Tell You." *Ladies' Home Journal*, Apr. 1994, 106–.

8. F. Fujita, E. Diener, and E. Sandvik, "Gender Differences in Negative Affect and Well-Being: The Case For Emotional Intensity." *Journal of Personality and Social Psychology*, 1991, 61, 3, 427–434.

9. Strong sex differences are found in throwing distance and accuracy, and in cognitive spatial rotation abilities necessary to aim moving projectiles at moving targets. R. Ashmore, "Sex, Gender, and the Individual." In L. Pervin (ed.), *Handbook of personality: Theory and research* (New York: Guilford Press, 1990) 486–526; and Buss, 1995, 166.

Chapter 9: Expressers and Fixers

1. L. Rubin, *Just friends: The role of friendship in our lives.* (New York: Harper & Row, 1985).

2. Tannen, 1990, 49–73.

3. See Tannen, 1990, 96–122.

4. G. Murdock, "The Common Denominator of Cultures." In G. Murdock, *Culture and Society* (Pittsburgh: Pittsburgh University Press, 1945); R. Wright, 1994, 236–262.

5. K. Hill and H. Kaplan, "Trade-Offs in Male and Female Reproductive Strategies Among the Ache, parts 1 and 2" (esp. 282–83). In L. Betzig, M. B. Mulder, and P. Turke (eds.) *Human Reproductive Behavior: A Darwinian Perspective* (New York: Cambridge University Press, 1988).

6. Frans de Waal, "Sex Differences in the Formation of Coalitions Among Chimpanzees." *Ethology and Sociobiology*, 5, 1984, 239–55 ; J. Goodall, *The Chimpanzees of Gombe: Patterns of Behavior* (Cambridge, Mass.: Harvard University Press, 1986).

7. Quoted in Symons, 1979, 162: see Wright, 1994, 248.

8. B. Low, "Cross-Cultural Patterns in the Training of Children: An Evolutionary Perspective." *Journal of Comparative Psychology*, 103, 1989, 311–319: reported in Archer, 1996, 915.

9. Peg Tyre, The trouble with boys. *Newsweek*, Jan 30, 2006, p. 44-52.

10. Comment credited to psychiatrist and media analyst Frank Pittman.

Part IV: Backwards into the Future

Chapter 10: The Rise and Fall of Fatherhood

1. S. Begley, " Beyond stones and bones." *Newsweek*, March 19, 2007, p. 57.

2. Suggested by P. Draper and H. Harpending, "A Sociobiological Perspective on the Development of Human Reproductive Strategies." In K.B. MacDonald (ed.), *Sociobiological Perspectives on Human Development* (New York: Springer-Verlag, 1988), 349.

3. Ken Wilber, *A Brief History of Everything.* Boston: Shambhala, 1996, p.46. Steven Pinker lists "group living" as a requisite for the evolution of higher intelligence, but not marriage specifically. In *How the Mind Works.* New York: Norton, 1997, p.192-4.

4. Jane Lancaster and Chet Lancaster, "The Watershed: Change in Parental Investment and Family Formation Strategies in the Course of Human Evolution." In J. Lancaster et al., eds., *Parenting Across the Life Span* (NY: Aldine de Gruyter, 1987), 189. See comments by Blankenhorn, *Fatherless America*, 25.

5. See Jared Diamond, *Guns, Germs, and Steel*, 1999, on farming.

6. J. Gottman, *The Seven Principles for Making Marriage Work*. p. 99-116.

7. Bernadette Gray-Little, and N. Burks, "Power and Satisfaction in Marriage." *Psychological Bulletin*, 933, 1983, 513–38; R.G. Corrales, "Power and Satisfaction in Early Marriage." In R.E. Cromwell and D.H. Olson (eds.), *Power in Families* (New York: Wiley, 1975); R. Centers, B.H. Raven, and A. Rodrigues, "Conjugal Power Structure: A Reexamination." *American Sociological Review*, 36, 1971, 264–278; R.O. Blood Jr. and D.M. Wolfe, *Husbands and Wives: The Dynamics of Married Living* (Glencoe, IL: Free Press, 1960).

8. Furstenberg, Jr. "Good Dads—Bad Dads: Two Faces of Fatherhood," in A. Cherlin (Ed.), *The Changing American Family and Public Policy* (D.C.: Urban Institute Press, 1998), 195. As cited in Maggie Gallagher, *The Abolition of Marriage*, 178-179.

9. Anna Quindlen, "Public and Private Men at Work." *New York Times*, 18 Feb. 1990, 19.

10. 1. Sanders Korenman and David Neumark, *Does Marriage Really Make Men More Productive?* Finance and Economics Discussion Series #29 (Washington DC, Division of Research and Statistics, Federal Reserve Board, May, 1988). As cited in Gallagher, 1996.

11. U.S. Bureau of Justice Statistics, *Highlights from 20 Years of Surveying Crime Victims: The National Crime Victimization Survey, 1973-92* (Washington, DC: US Department of Justice, 1993), 18. Statistics includes females 12 and older. See also D. Blankenhorn, *Fatherless America*, 32-42.

12. See: David Crary, "Cohabitation called dangerous to children." *AP*, Nov. 18, 2007.

13. Blankenhorn also sees an alliance with the mother and physical presence in the family as the two essential conditions for an inseminator to be a good enough father. See *Fatherless America*.

14. Steven Pinker, *How the Mind Works* (NY: Norton, 1997), p. 432.

15. See Daniel Amneus. *The Garbage Generation: The Consequences of the Destruction of the Two-Parent Family and the Need to Stabilize It by Strengthening its Weakest Link, the Father's Role*. (Alhambra, CA: Primrose Press, 1990).

Chapter 11: Primal Passions in a Changing World

Index

Index

Index

Index

Index

Index

Acknowledgments

Thanks to Keith Davis and Peter Ossorio, for introducing us to ordinary language psychology;

Thanks to our many friends and colleagues who offered sage comments and sharpened our focus, and to our academic colleagues for reviewing our evolutionary psychology;

And finally, Driscoll offers a special thanks to Nancy Ann Davis, my wife and colleague and close confidant for over three decades, for her continuing involvement with this project.

the Authors

Richard Driscoll, Ph.D., specializes in relationship therapy, anxiety reduction, and spiritual concerns. He is a media resource with the American Psychological Association and has contributed to various publications including Oprah.com .

Contributing author Nancy Ann Davis, Ph.D., specializes in relationships and in helping women balance family and careers.

Driscoll and Davis are married, have three grown children, and are in clinical practice together.

While we do see couples together, the "we" in the text may refer to either one of our experiences, so long as we both agree with the observations.